BAS   LL
DRILLS

WITH ACKNOWLEDGMENT AND THANKS TO COACH TONY GARBELOTT FOR HIS CONTRIBUTIONS AND ALSO TO MY COLLEAGUES AT THE U.K. BASKETBALL ACADEMY.

INTRODUCTION

Included in this booklet are drills which I have used over the years at all levels and have found them to be either very useful and effective or simply a means of adding change and variety to practice.

There is no short cut to mastering the fundamentals . . . it is a matter of intense and constant repetition.

But remember, practice alone is useless, only perfect practice is productive. You must insist that your players (a) work hard with intensity at all times and (b) perform and execute the skill(s) properly.

There are many other drills that are used all over the world apart from the ones contained in this book; you should be innovative in devising some of your own drills that may suit you, your personnel and/or your situation.

In my experience the things to ensure are: keep the drills simple; explain and/or demonstrate quickly and concisely; insist on correct execution and intensity; try to involve as many players as possible; be aware of safety and prevention of injury.

Basketball is the greatest game on earth, played by the best athletes, it is up to you, the Coach, to instill and promote the correct attitudes in your players.

This book of drills will help you with some ideas and also with organisation which is a key to doing your job well.

Coach Mark W. Dunning

A Coach's Guide to Drills for the Fundamentals of Basketball

– – – – – →	PASS
————————→	PLAYER MOVEMENT
∿∿∿∿∿∿⇀	DRIBBLE
–·–·–·–·→	SHOT
X1	DEFENSIVE PLAYER
O1	OFFENSIVE PLAYER
—————————⊣	SCREEN
⋀⋀⋀⋀⋀⋀↝	DEFENSIVE SLIDE
↶↷	POST UP

CONTENTS

FOOTWORK

Triple Threat Position

Hands in the "T" catch position on the ball.

Ball in "shooting pocket."

Face the basket.

Knees bent, head up, weight slightly on balls of feet, shooting foot slightly forward. (The Basketball Position!)

1. Spin the ball out (using backward rotation) for yourself and assume the triple threat position on catching it.

   Do this in several locations around the court.

2. Have the ball passed to the player from different angles and places, player catches the ball and assumes the triple threat position (always FACING THE BASKET.)

Individual Offensive Moves with the Ball

1. Before making any offensive move with the ball assume the triple threat position.

2. Practice all moves with both left and right hands. (I used to teach players to also practice all moves using their left *and* right foot as a pivot foot, however, in recent years I have advocated the teaching of *only* using your dominant pivot foot i.e. the left foot for right handers and right foot for lefties!).

3. Practice all moves from right side, left side and in front of the basket.

The Moves

1. Ball fake/pump fake — a short, quick movement of the ball in one direction, followed by, quickly and in the same motion a pass, pivot, shot or dribble in another direction. (Pump fake is used usually to fake a shot when underneath the basket to make the defender "leave his feet").

2. Head and shoulder fake — Either before a shot or dribble.

3. Jab step and drive — (Protect ball on opposite hip.) Jab the foot (outside) past the defender, one dribble, lay up.

4. Short jab, jab extend and drive — as for 3. except first jab is only about 6" in front, then without bringing foot back, extend the jab step, one dribble, lay up.

5. Crossover step and drive — (Protect ball on opposite hip.) Bring foot and leg across the body's mid-line (and across the defender, thus "sealing him"), one dribble, lay up.

6. Jab 6", crossover and and drive — short jab with right foot to the right, swing ball through on left hip, crossover step with right foot to left side, one dribble left hand, lay up.

8

7. Rocker step	– Player steps towards basket as if to drive, as defender retreats (if he doesn't, the offensive player should continue to basket), offensive player draws back his foot, straightens up as if to shoot, if defender comes forward, offensive player thrusts his foot towards the basket again and drives for the lay up.
8. Fake drive & shoot	– Player goes as if to drive, defender reacts, player pulls back and takes a jump shot.
9. Fake shot and drive	– Ball fake as if to shoot, defender reacts by straightening take the ball in on the drive.

N.B. ONE good fake and then a strong move is usually more effective than several weak fakes.

10. Jab and shoot	– Fake directly at the defender and shoot over him.
11. Jab and go	– "Stutter step" at the defender and explode by him for the lay up.
12. Jab, go & power	– Fake and drive past the defender then stop at the basket and explode straight up to the rim off two feet. (Jump stop.)
13. Go over for jumper	– One "escape" dribble to the right and shoot jumper.
14. Jab, hesitation dribble & go	– Jab fake, make a hesitation dribble and go in for lay up.
15. Jab & reverse	– Jab fake, drive to basket and go underneath for right hand lay up.
16. Jab & reverse opposite	– As for 15, but use left hand to shoot.
17. Drive & spin	– Dribble towards the baseline then spin dribble into and across lane for lay up or hook shot.

18. Jab & go across — Dribble right side of court, jab fake then dribble across the lane for the lay up.

19. Go across for jumper — Drive hard right to left for the jump shot.

20. Go across, hesitation — Drive hard right to left, hesitation dribble and drive in for lay up.

21. Go across and spin — Drive right to left, use spin dribble when "cut-off" and go in for right hand lay up.

22. Go across, fake spin and go — As for 21, except fake the spin dribble and continue for left hand lay up.

Drills

1. 1 on 1 with passive defence: Defensive player "checks" ball to commence the action.

2. 1 on 1 live action: Use only moves outlined.

Diagrams 1–3 show the organization for moves 1–9.
Diagram 4 shows the organization for moves 10–22.

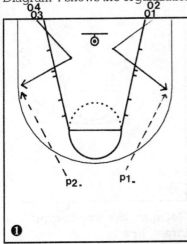

❶

Players O1 & O3 V cut & signal
for ball. Players P1 & P2 make a
good pass. O1 & O3 get into
triple threat position.

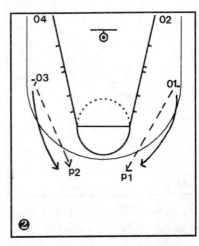

❷

O1 & O3 pass back to P1 & P2,
they assume triple threat
position. O1 & O3 follow pass
and receive a hand-off from
P1/P2.

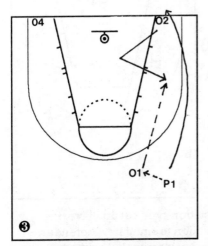

❸

O1 & O3 triple threat, P1/P2
join back of line. Meanwhile O2
& O4 are on their V cuts.
Change sides every minute.

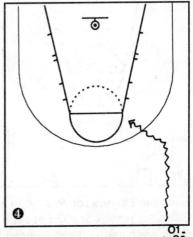

❹

Players begin at mid-court &
dribble in to perform each
move. Change sides either after
each shot or after 3 minutes.

11

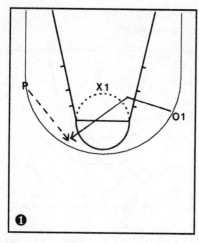

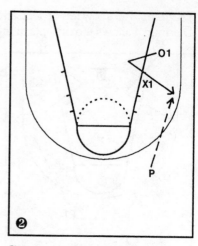

Entry pass then 1 on 1. The pass can be made from any position.

Get open, entry pass, triple threat, 1 on 1.

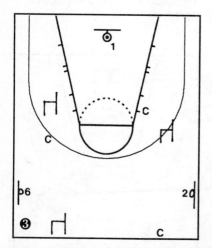

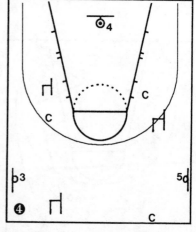

Have the Players rotate around a station-type set up. have one Coach or player or chair at each station to simulate a defender. Each hoop has a number, each number designates a different move, e.g.. No.1=jab, crossover & drive. Players must perform twice at each hoop. Left & right sides.

Footwork and Individual Offence without the Ball

For helping to improve footwork speed/quickness, jump rope! It also helps coordination and is a good conditioner. (There are various combinations that can be practised).

The following should be taught:

1. V cuts – towards basket and away from basket.
2. L cuts.
3. Backdoor cut.
4. One count jump stop.
5. Triple threat position, emphasis on having feet pointing towards the basket, ready with shooting foot forward.
6. Reverse pivot.
7. Front pivot.
8. Inside pivot for post play.
9. Drop step for post play.
10. Pick and roll. Open towards ball.
11. Defensive footwork.
12. Footwork for lay ups.
13. Spin moves for post player "in the paint".

Two Important Drills

1. TWO ON TWO: (i) No dribbling; emphasis on V cuts, L cuts.
   Getting open.
   Cutting to hoop.
   (ii) Dribbling allowed; emphasis on the above plus, pick & roll on ball.

2. THREE ON THREE: (i) No dribbling; emphasis on the above plus, pick & roll away from the ball.
   (ii) Dribbling; all the above.

Also incorporated into the two drills can be emphasis on pivoting and inside (post) moves.

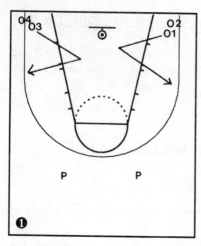

①

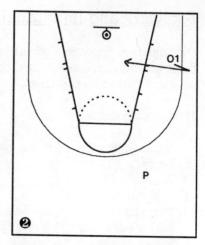

②

Phantom.
Players make good V cuts. Pop out (create a lead), receive phantom pass from P, assume triple threat position, swap sides.

Backdoor Cut. Phantom Series.
As before, except player imagines a defender is over-playing him so he makes a backdoor cut. Receives imaginary pass.

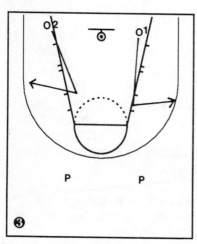

③

④

Phantom L Cuts Drill.
As for V cuts.

Phantom Pick & Roll.
O1 down screens for O2 (and rolls).
O2 uses screen topside, receives pass from P and triple threat. Emphasise footwork for O1 & O2.

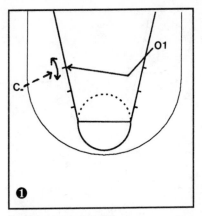

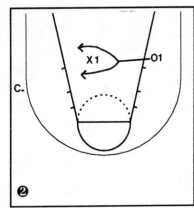

Inside & Outside Pivots.

Do both sides of lane. No defence at first, then with a defender. Player receives ball and comes to a one count jump stop outside the paint. (Baseline foot is no lower than second hash mark). Perform the pivot, first with left and then with right foot.

Then perform drop steps – baseline first then into paint.

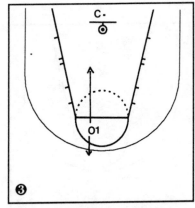

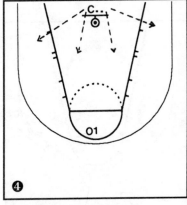

Quick Reaction Footwork Drill.

Player must go out to touch top of circle each time. O1 runs in and Coach passes him the ball, at varying points within the lane. Coach yells "right, left, front, jump". Player must react and perform right hand layup, lefty lay up, dunk or front rim layup or jump shot.

Quick Reaction Footwork Conditioner.

As previous except Coach will have two or three basketballs and will throw them out with little interval. Player must catch ball before it bounces twice. Can introduce more commands.

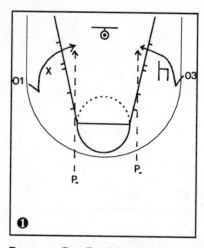

①

②

Reverse Cut (Backdoor) Drill.

Use chairs or stationary defensive players. Concentrate on correct footwork. Players change sides each time.

Fake Reverse & Inside Cut Drill

As previous, except jab fake the backdoor cut and cut inside and to the basket.

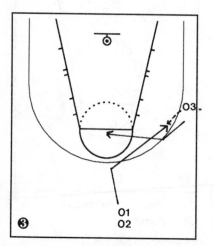

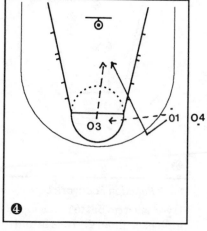

③

④

V Cuts/L Cuts Drill

O1 V cuts towards O3 and comes to one count jump stop. O3 makes hand-off and cuts off O1's outside shoulder. O1 makes reverse pivot and gets into triple threat. O3 makes one count stop and reverse pivot, O1 passes to O3 and cuts to hoop. O3 passes to O1 for lay up.

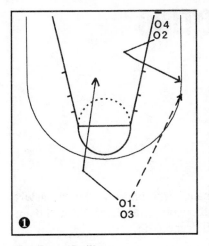 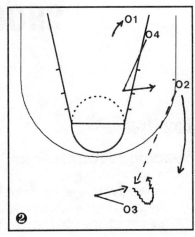

Get Open Drill

O1 triple threat. O2 L cut. O1 pass to O2 (triple threat). O1 V cut, O2 fake pass. O3 is in motion now V cutting and replacing. O2 pass to O3. O3 back dribble up as O4 is on his L cut. Repeat and rotate (as shown).

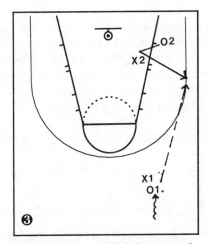

Progression – add defence and allow a shot or 1 on 1 action.

SHOOTING

Lay Ups

Teaching Progressions

(i) Left side of basket, ball in left hand, hand underneath the ball with the fingers spread, wrist and elbow underneath the ball and pointing at the basket, ball on top of left shoulder.

Stand approx. 2' away from the basket, left side of the rim, bend knees, aim for top left corner of little square.

Extend knees, extend left elbow and push ball onto backboard.

(ii) As (i) except now stand on one leg! (Right leg for left handed shot on left side), extend & shoot.

(iii) Stand on second hash mark of free throw lane, feet together, take two steps and say out loud, "Left foot, right foot, shoot!".
Players will have the ball above left shoulder, left hand underneath ball, head looking up at target. Foot sequence must be in correct order (left foot, then right foot, jump and shoot.) MUST shoot with LEFT hand from left side.

(iv) Step back, take one dribble then "left foot, right foot, shoot!".

(v) Progress to taking 2, 3, 4 or more dribbles, take the two steps and shoot the lay up.

REPEAT ALL DRILLS FOR THE RIGHT HAND LAY UP.

Foot sequence will now be "Right foot, left foot, shoot!". Shoot with the right hand.

Perform all drills from left and right sides.

Two lane lay up drill

Use 2 balls, begin both lines behind 10 sec. line. First player in shooting line dribbles in and shoots the lay up; at the same time O5 from rebounding line runs in to collect ball, dribbling out and passes to next player O3. O1 joins rebounding line.

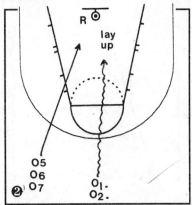

As before but shooting line is in the middle of the floor. Rebounder joins shooting line after passing ball to next player.

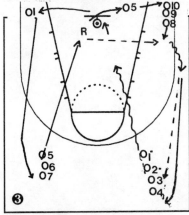

Two lane lay ups with pass.

As before, except the rebounder makes a pass to O8 who has stepped in. O8 passes to O3 & joins the back of the line. O5 joins passing line.

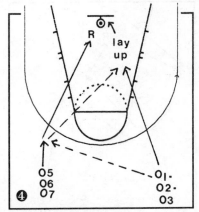

Two pass lay up drill.

Rotation and organization as for previous drills, except the lay up is made off a pass. Encourage good footwork, timing & passing.

19

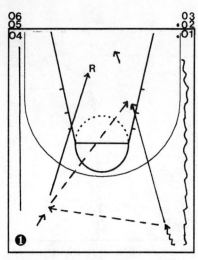

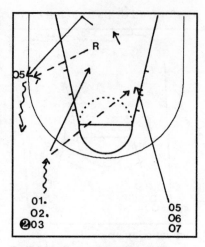

Dribble, 2 pass lay up drill.
Players dribble up sideline
with outside hand, perform spin
or reverse dribble at 10 sec.
line. Meanwhile O4 runs hard to
10 sec. line, makes reverse
pivot & comes in ready to pass
& rebound.

Dribble, lay up, outlet drill.
O1 will dribble in some of the
way, then pass to O5. O5 will
perform a right hand lay up. O1
will rebound & make an outlet
pass to O5 who has cut to the
outlet pass area. O1 join
shooting line, O5 join passing

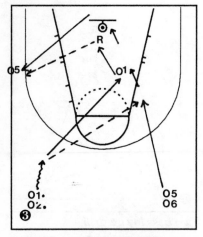

Dribble, lay up, outlet with
defence.
As above but O1 will give some
defensive pressure to O5 who
must make the lay up.

20

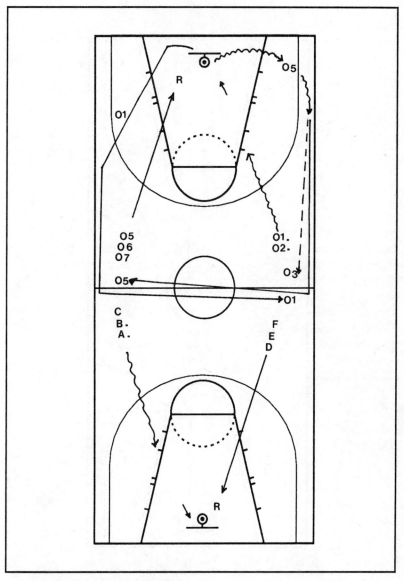

Full Court Figure 8 Lay Up Drill.

You shoot the lay up in one end, run up the sideline, along 10 sec.
line and join the rebounding line at the other end.

Two balls going at each end at the same time.

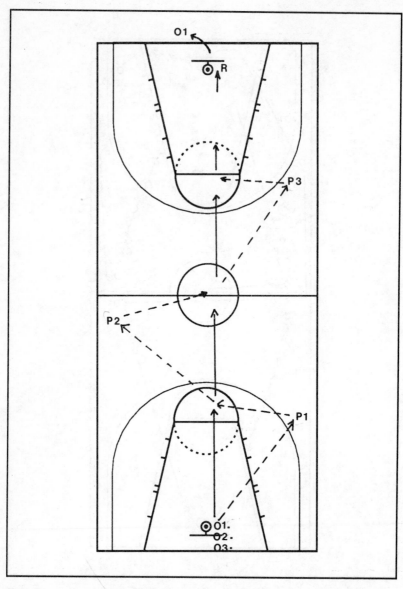

Full Court, Pass & Lay Up Drill.

O1 passes to P1, cuts up the middle of the court & receives pass back, passes to P2, cuts & gets it back, pass to P3, gets it back & makes the lay up. Meantime, O2 & O3 etc. have started doing the same.

Change direction after several minutes.

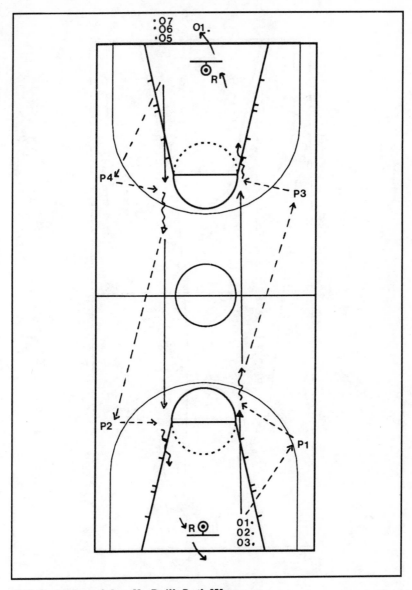

Full Court Pass & Lay Up Drill, Both Ways.

Change direction and passers after several minutes.

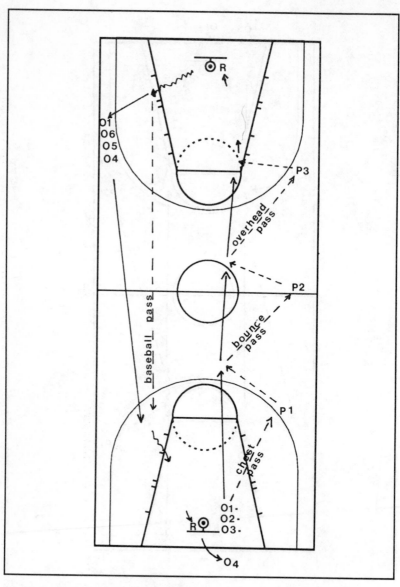

Multi-Purpose Pass & Lay Up Drill.

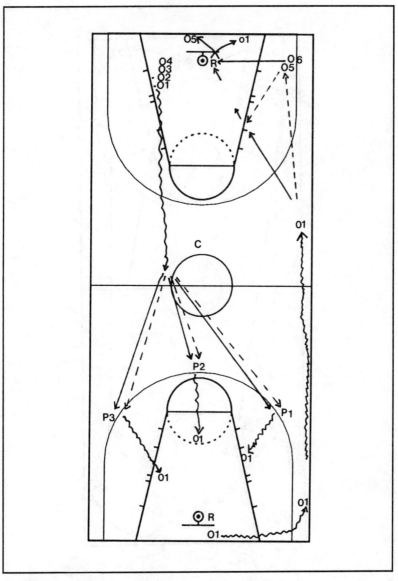

Heads Up Drill with Lay Ups.

Coach has his back to players. As O1 goes past Coach, Coach will point to one of the passers. That player signals towards O1 who immediately makes the pass, & cuts towards him. He receives hand-off & drives in for the lay up. Gets rebound & dribbles back, passes to O5, gets it back, lay it up. O5 rebound & swap lines.

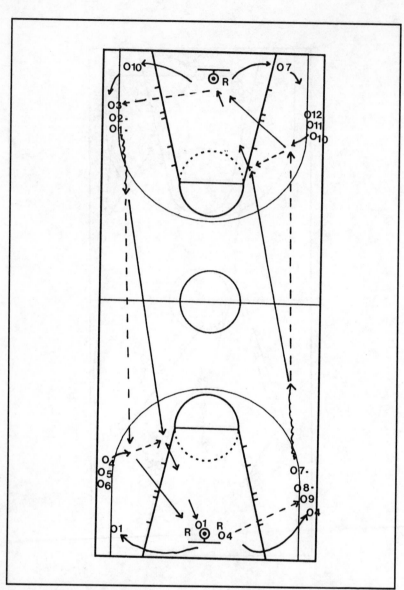

Four Corner Lay Up Drill.

Divide the players into the 4 corners of the court. O1, O2, O7, O8 have basketballs. O1 & O7 begin at the same time. O4 & O10 will cut in & signal for the ball. O1 & O7 will pass & follow their pass. Receive the ball from O4 & O10 will make a lay up & join the passing line. O4 & O10 will rebound, outlet the ball to O3 & O9 and join the shooting line.

Change direction after a few minutes.

26

Shooting — the Jump Shot

Regardless of what else takes place on court, accurate shooting is a must if a team is to become and remain a strong contender. First shots are critical so it is very important for players to establish correct shooting habits from the very beginning of their basketball careers.

Good shooters are developed not born. It is doubtful that there has ever been a great shooter who did not require countless hours of practice to develop his proficiency.

The shooter must concentrate on the target area, the point on the rim or backboard at which he is sighting – before, during AND AFTER the shot (the ball being released). Failure to concentrate on the target is a common fault among many players. Be on the alert to correct it.

Among the fundamental skills is knowing when to shoot. All players love to shoot and to their minds, seldom take a bad shot! It is the Coach's difficult task to be sure each player comes to know the floor areas from which he can shoot with a good "winning" percentage of made shots and the phases of the team offence from which those shots will be obtained.

What makes a shot hit?
1. Body balance and control.
2. Stance.
3. Grip.
4. Position of elbow.
5. Position of the ball before release.
6. Sighting the basket and target areas.
7. Release of ball.
8. Force behind the shot.
9. Follow through.
10. Flight arc of the ball.
11. Concentration.

"DON'T PRACTICE SHOOTING, PRACTICE MAKING SHOTS".

Mechanics

1 FEET
The feet should be pointing at the target (the rim). The shooting foot (i.e.. same foot as the shooting hand) slightly forward. Feet not too wide apart, nor too close – whatever is comfortable. Weight on balls of feet.

2 KNEES

When getting ready to shoot, knees should be bent. On jumping the use of the legs is extremely vital. Ankles, then gastrocnemius muscle initiate vertical force, knees straighten, then quadriceps and hamstring muscles come into play.

3 HIPS

Should be facing the target, i.e.. square to the basket.

4 HEAD AND SHOULDERS

Shoulders should be square and facing target. Head still and not leaning backwards or sideways . . . especially during and after release.

5 EYES

Should be fixed on the target. BEFORE, DURING AND AFTER the shot – do NOT look at the ball in flight.

Target = whatever you have success with. I teach, net hook at the back of the rim! Find a target you like and stick with it thereafter!

6 SHOOTING ARM

Position of the elbow will depend on your natural swing. (Swing arm by your side and lift it up as if to prepare to shoot). Your elbow should be pointing at the target and be underneath your wrist. (An angle of about 45° should be made from armpit to basket, between this imaginary line and the line of elbow to basket). Your elbow will be underneath the ball.

7 WRIST

Cocked back and underneath the ball, pointing at the target.

8 THUMB

Two-thirds of the bottom part is on the ball (not flat on the ball because this causes less flexibility in the wrist).

9 FINGERS

Spread the fingers on the underneath of the ball. The ball should rest on the pads of the fingers – never the palm. The span, i.e. the distance between the tip of the thumb and the tip of the little finger is all important.

10 POSITION OF BALL

At this stage the ball should be in the "shooting pocket" (triple threat position). The shooting pocket is located just above armpit level.

11 NON-SHOOTING HAND

Hand is on the side of the ball, simply for support of the ball. This hand DOES NOT take part in the shot, other than to give support to the ball.

12 RELEASE OF SHOT

Analogy; you are in a telephone booth, shoot the ball through the roof. Position of the ball – on jumping, the ball will come to above and slightly in front of the forehead. There are two types of jump shot; One motion jump shot = jump and shoot at the same time. Two motion jump shot = jump, then shoot at the top of the jump.

13 STRAIGHTENING OF THE ELBOW

There should be a straight line on release of the ball from the armpit through the elbow to the plane of the basket. (Not underneath the background or over it). Elbow should be still pointing towards the basket – not out to one side.

14 SNAP OF WRIST

This will ensure good follow-through and feel/touch. "Wave goodbye to the ball". "Try to put your hand into the basket from above the rim".

15 FOLLOW-THROUGH

Arm first, wrist second, then fingers.

16 FINGERS

Spread the hand. The index finger and middle two fingers are the important ones. The ball leaves these two fingers last and it must come off the tips of them.

17 SHOOTING POCKET TO RELEASE

With most people the thumb will follow a line through the nose, and the forefinger will follow a line through the ear!

18 FLIGHT OF THE BALL

The ball should have some reverse rotation and should travel in a fairly high arc to the basket. (You can fit two basketballs side by side into the rim!). Don't watch the ball in flight.

19 AFTER THE SHOT

Land on the same spot that you took off from. Don't fade away. Feet should still be pointing at the rim. Don't jump forward. 'Freeze' your follow-through position for a short while so as to encourage and reinforce good form.

20 NON-SHOOTING HAND

Should be still in the position neat to your ("snapped") shooting hand.

Drills

1 PHANTOM SHOOTING DRILL

Players position themselves around the lane area, Coach is under the basket facing players; Coach slaps ball, players are in 'ready' position, on the slap they shoot an imaginary jump shot. "Think the ball into the basket". Players must follow-through and quickly get ready for the next shot. Stay low, feet pointing at the target, eyes remain fixed on target. Check form.

2 PHANTOM DRILL WITH SHOOTER

As 1, but Coach will pass the ball to somebody, he shoots the ball, at the same time everyone else shoots a phantom shot. (Can have 'penalties' if shot is missed).

3 PHANTOM DRIBBLE, SHOT

Players take one phantom dribble right, up and shoot. NB. Inside foot = left foot for right handed shooter, steps, then right foot comes around, brakes with inside of shoe, a little in front of the left foot, up and shoot.

Then, one phantom dribble left etc. (Left foot when coming round brakes a little behind shooting foot).

4 CHECK BALL SPIN

Using just shooting hand, stand facing the the rim, simply push the ball vertically into the air (using correct follow-through of elbow, wrist snap, fingers etc.). Ball should return to hand without player having to move. (Can also be done facing a wall, start with feet about 6" away from wall).

5 BANK SHOOTING

Players line up on either side of the lane and take bank shots. Rebound own shot, pass to next player in the line and join the other side.

6 QUICK RELEASE

In pairs, non-shooter has ball at arm's length out in front of him. Shooter takes ball off partner's hand. As soon as shooter takes ball, non-shooter puts a hand up 'in shooter's face'. Shooter works on form.

7 SQUARE-UP AND SHOOT
Coach stands at top of the lane, player makes cuts to different spots, receives ball from Coach, squares up and shoots. Rebounds ball, passes back to Coach, goes to different spot, receives ball, repeat. Check form.

8 START CLOSE – WORK OUT
Start in close to the hoop, take 10–12 shots, take one step back, take 10–12 shots, take another step back etc. Work on form. Try and go for "swishes" i.e. ball goes through without touching the rim.

9 DEAN SMITH DRILL
Shoot the ball back and forth to each other. (Pairs about 15' apart). Observe each other's form – coach each other. Target is your partner's forehead.

"Become your own shooting coach".

10 SHOOT 25
In pairs, the non-shooter is stationary at the top of the lane, shooter receives pass from partner, shoots the jumper, gets own rebound, passes back to partner, moves to a different spot receives ball, shoots etc. Shoot 25 shots.

11 SHOOT 25 WITH DRIBBLE
As 10, but with one dribble before the shot. Left, right, straight ahead.

12 SHOOT 25 WITH DRIBBLE MOVE
As above except with a dribble move to get you the shot. (e.g. Spin dribble, behind the back dribble etc.).

13 BEAT THE PRO
(Player chooses an imaginary opponent to play against). Shoot a free throw, if you miss, Pro gets 3 points. If you make it you get 1 point. Shoot perimeter jump shots, every shot you miss Pro gets 2 points, every shot you make you get 1 point. Play until either you or the Pro reaches 11 points.

14 21 SHOOTING DRILL

Can be done in pairs or in teams of 3/4. Perform from various areas of the floor. First player shoots and follows his shot. If he scores he gets 2 points, if he can catch the ball before it hits the floor and make the lay up (only one attempt allowed) he gets another point = 3. If he shoots and misses but manages to catch the ball before it hits the floor and make the lay up = 1 point. If he shoots and scores but can't catch the rebound before it hits the floor = 2 points. Pass to next guy in line, or partner, who does the same from the same spot. First team to 21 points wins.

15 TEAM SHOOTING

Divide the team into e.g. 5 or 6 players at each end, with 3 basketballs per team. Everyone shoots and everyone rebounds (shots must be from outside the lane). Keep score, when they hear the whistle blow they must dribble the basketballs and get them and all the team to the other end of the court where they continue shooting and continue their score. First team to make 25 baskets wins. Every time whistle blows, change ends.

16 CLOSE OUT ON SHOT

In pairs. Non-shooter passes the ball into shooter from baseline. Follows his pass and runs the first couple of steps then slides the last two with his inside hand and foot up, i.e. the hand and foot nearest the basket. Gets a hand up on the shot, yells "Shot!" and boxes out, shooter tries to follow shot go get rebound. 5 and rotate.

17 PAIRS FULL COURT

In pairs behind the baseline players go full speed up the floor whilst making good chest passes, at the other end one of the players pulls up and takes a jump shot, the non-shooter rebounds. Go for time or certain number of baskets to be made.

Pressure Shooting

1 FORM

It is vital that you maintain good and proper form throughout your shot. Don't fade, don't jump forward. Don't 'force' the shot.

2 QUICK RELEASE

Don't hold the ball low down where the defence can slap it away. Don't 'wind yourself up' to shoot, i.e. tell the defence that you are going to shoot. Get the shot off quick but don't rush it.

3 CONCENTRATION

Don't be put off by a hand in your face or the slap on your arm or body, or a distraction in the crowd. Concentrate on THE TARGET throughout the shot.

4 WORK HARD

To get open, to get a good shot. To jump & shoot.

5 RANGE

You must know your range, know what is a good shot for you to take. Try to get open within your 'shooting range'.

6 PERCENTAGE

It's important to know from which spots on the floor you can hit the best percentage (but with pressure).

Further your knowledge – discover also *"The Ultimate Shooting Method"*.

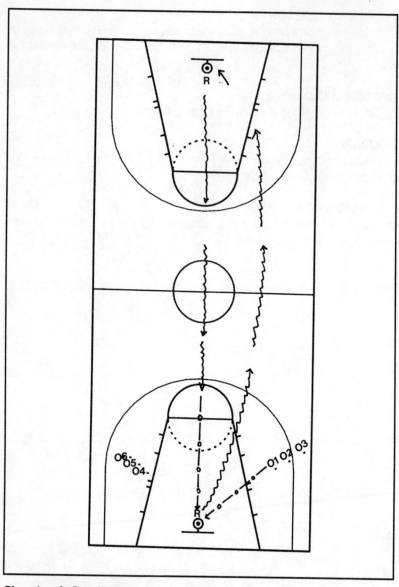

Shooting & Conditioner.

O1 shoots, gets own rebound, dribbles to the other end, gets lay up, dribbles back, shoots the J from top of lane, gets rebound, passes to team mate who does the same.

First team to 21

Max. 3 pts for all 3 shots made.

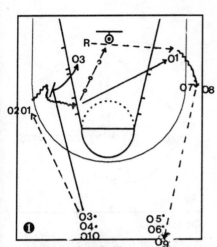

Pass, Pick , Pop Drill

O3 passes to O1 and picks for him. O1 dribbles off screen and shoots. O3 rebounds and passes to O1 who has cleared opposite. O1 passes to O9. Players rotate to the OPPOSITE line after each shot, i.e. O1 goes behind O9 & O3 goes behind O8. O7 & O5 are doing the same thing at the same time.

Square Up & Shoot.

Pass to the passer (P), V cut to bank shot angle, get ball back, square up, shoot, collect ball, join other line. Keep P working hard by passing quickly from alternate sides.

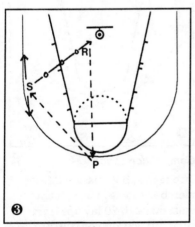

Two Ball Shooting.

One man shoot, one man rebound, one man pass. Take 10 & rotate.

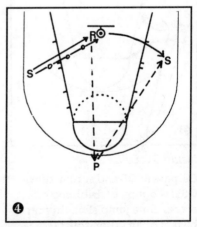

Pairs Shooting With Pass.

Shoot, get own rebound, pass to partner, go to different spot, receive ball, shoot . . . 10 & rotate.

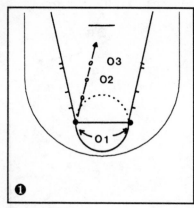

① *Pick Up & Shoot.*

Pick the balls up from the elbows. Shoot the jumper. 2 other players rebound and replace balls. Work for one minute or certain number of made shots.

② *Shoot to 100.*

Try to shoot 100 made shots in five minutes or less. O1 makes hard cut to the ball. O4 pass & join the opposite line. O1 rebound own shot, pass to next player in shooting line & go to back of that line.

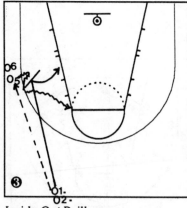

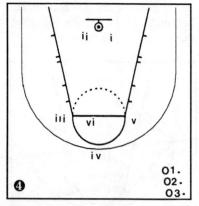

③ *Inside Out Drill.*

O1 pass to O5 and screen down. O5 has option of dribbling off screen for a jump shot, driving to basket or hit O1 on roll. O1 rebounds & outlets to O5 – change sides.

④ *Competition Shooting.*

Two teams, both baskets. Each member shoots in turn, team must make (i) 20 lay ups from right, (ii) 20 from left, (iii) 10 jump shots left, (iv) 10 jump shots top, (v) 10 from right (iv) 20 free throws. First team to complete all shots is the winner.

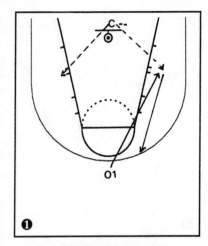

❶

"Iron Man" Shooting Drill.

Coach is under the hoop with 2 basketballs – Coach throws them out one at a time anywhere – player must catch the ball after only one bounce. Coach yells "1" = lay up, "2" = jumper, "3" = power dribble & jumper, "4" = pass fake & go. Work for one minute or number of made shots.

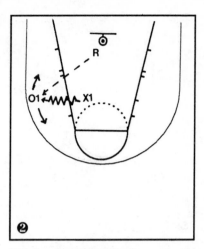

❷

"Bother the Shot" Drill.

One player shoot, one player rebounds and passes, the other player bothers the shot. Take 10 and rotate.

❸

"Billy The Kid" Drill.

O1 dribbles up and down the court – FULL SPEED shooting jumpers from outside the lane. He receives a pass from two rebounders (one at each end) INSIDE the 3 point line. Go for 10 made shots.

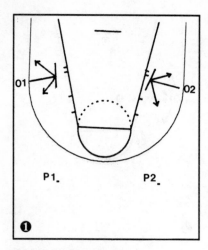

❶

2 Man Screen-Shot.
Use two balls, screener flares
out towards guard spots or
baseline.

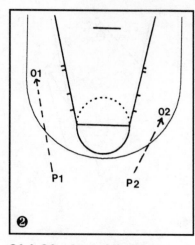

❷

O1 & O2 rebound their own
shots and join the passing lines.
P1 & P2 join the shooting lines.

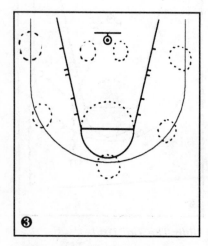

❸

Against the clock shooting drill.

Player must shoot and dribble
out to next spot. Aim is to try
and score from each spot. (2 pts
each).

SCORE = total time minus 10 pts.

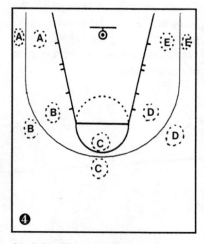

❹

2's & 3's Shooting Drill.

In pairs, one rebounder, alternate shooting a 2 pointer then a
3 from specified areas. Race
(e.g.) – make from each spot.

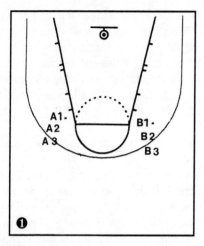

"4 Up" Shooting Drill.

Two teams, one ball each team. Take it in turn to shoot from designated areas. Count in 1's. Team A is trying to get 4 made baskets up on Team B.

Must keep count out loud, or Coach/Manager can keep score. Rebound your own shot & pass to next teamate in line.

Free Throw Shooting

1. RHYTHM – bounce ball, take deep breath.
2. REPETITION.
3. ONE STYLE – stick to it.
4. KNEES – bend them.
5. FOLLOW THROUGH.
6. FLIGHT OF BALL – high arc, swish it!
7. TARGET – back of rim (?). Whatever YOU sight.
8. CONCENTRATION – free throws are VERY IMPORTANT.

Drills

Shoot free throws after trying drills and after practice.
1. Shoot 6,8,9 in a row before you go; if you miss, run a sprint.
2. In pairs, shoot two and rotate. Target number . . .
3. In teams, shoot 25. Each player will shoot two and rotate.

4. Shoot for suicides: Everyone takes it in turn to shoot 2 free throws. Can either do this in two teams or as a whole squad in one basket. If the whole squad (or one team) can shoot 80% then they don't have to run any suicides at the end of practice.

5. Make 'em or drill it: Each player steps in turn to make two foul shots. Each time someone misses one or two the whole squad has some form of penalty or forfeit (e.g. pairs fundamentals drill).

6. In threes, shoot two and rotate: Each one you miss run a 9 sec. full court sprint.

7. Shoot for the team: One team at each end, players step up to line for 2 shots, if they miss the whole team runs a full court sprint. Can target a specific number or go for time.

8. Make 'em or run: Two and rotate × 3. If you miss your first shot = 1 full court sprint. If you make your first but miss your second = 2 full court sprints. If you miss them both = 3 full court sprints!

9. Swish 'em: Continuous 2 and rotate, target a number or go for time. If you swish the shot = 3 points. If you make it but it hits some rim = 2 points. If you make it but it rattles around the rim or hits the backboard first = 1 point!

BALL HANDLING & PASSING

Musts

1. Keep your head up at all times. Keep eyes up too.
2. Get a feel for the ball. Develop a soft touch.
3. Use your fingertips to control the ball, never your palm.
4. Exercise your wrists and fingers to keep them loose and flexible.
5. When you have mastered a drill/skill/technique, perform it at full speed – as fast as you can whilst maintaining full control.
6. Be able to perform equally well with both left and right hands.

Drills

1. BALL SLAP
Slap the ball as hard as you can with either hand. Spread your fingers.

2. PINCH BALL
'Pinch' the ball with right then left hand. Pinch it up in the air. Try and palm it with right hand then left hand.

3. BALL FLIP
Flip the ball back and forth between your fingertips over your head with arms fully extended. Keep it flipping and work your way down your body and up again.

4. BALL WEAVE
Rotate the ball around your head, waist and both knees together, then around right leg, then around left leg, ankles. Keep changing the direction of the rotation.

5. FIGURE EIGHT
Move the ball around your legs in a figure eight pattern as quickly as possible. Change direction.

6. FIGURE EIGHT DRIBBLE
As for 5, but use dribble. Change direction.

7. SCISSORS
Make scissors motion with legs (i.e. alternate feet front and back), whilst passing the ball through, e.g. Left leg is in front, ball goes from right hand to left hand; right leg comes in front, ball goes from left hand to right.

8. WALKING SCISSORS
Full court, as 7, except you are on the move baseline to baseline. Come back backwards.

9. WEAK HAND DRIBBLE
Dribble the ball with your weak hand around your weak leg.

10. WEAK HAND 2 BALL DRIBBLE
As 9, but occupy your strong hand by dribbling a second ball.

11. ONE BOUNCE AND THROUGH
Take one bounce with right hand at your right side then bounce ball through your legs (from front to back), control with left hand, one bounce left side, back through legs etc.

12. DRIBBLE SIT UPS
Dribble a ball whilst doing sit ups. Repeat for each hand.

13. TWO BALL DRIBBLE SIT UPS
Same as 12, but two balls at once.

14. KNEE DRIBBLE
While on one knee, dribble ball around your body including through your legs. Do on both hands/knees.

15. BEHIND BACK CATCH
Throw ball into the air and see how many times you can clap your hands before catching it behind your back. Toss it back over your head and repeat.

16. BALL SLAM
Slam the ball between your legs and catch it behind your back then toss it up to your head catching it behind your neck, bring it back over your head and slam it through again.

17. BEHIND THE BACK TOSS

With your right hand toss the ball from behind your back and catch it in front of your body. Ball shouldn't touch the other hand. Repeat with left hand.

18. BEHIND THE BACK OFF WALL

Throw behind the back passes off a wall with each hand.

19. DRIBBLE BALL WALK

As for you walk up and down the court, dribble the ball back and forth between legs. (Each time you take a step, dribble the ball through). Come back backwards.

20. CRADLE

Spread feet wide, back straight and knees bent. (Ball stays under buttocks). Right hand in front of ball and legs. Quickly switch position of hands, while keeping ball off the floor.

21. DOUBLE CRADLE

As 20, except both hands are in front together and in back together.

22. CLAP CATCH

Crouch down slightly, hold ball behind knees, clap hands in front and catch ball behind – before it hits the floor. (Don't flip the ball up!).

23. HIKE (or HUT)

Get in a stance similar to a football centre at the offensive line and toss the ball through legs and over your head, catch it in front.

24. SPIN IT

Put an even spin on the ball using either two hands or a flick of the wrist with one hand. After you can consistently find the balance point, change fingers, change hands, push the ball off one finger into the air and regain its balance again on one finger, bounce the spinning ball off your knee, elbow, head, foot and back to the finger. Keep ball rotating by 'slapping' it with the free hand.

25. RHYTHM DRILL

Stand with the knees flexed holding the ball with two hands in front of the body. Swing ball around right leg and bring to cradle position. Let it bounce and catch it with hands switched (left in back, right in front). With left hand take ball around left leg to original cradle position (left hand in front, right hand in back). Repeat and change direction.

26. WALKING RHYTHM
As for 25, only walk forward as fast as possible.

27. STANDING WINDMILL
Stand with legs spread and knees flexed. Ball is in front and between legs. Drop ball, dribble it with right hand then left hand in front. Now quickly dribble it with right hand then left hand behind legs. Repeat as fast as possible.

28. WALKING WINDMILL
As for 27, except walk up and down the court.

29. LAKER REACTION
Reacting man is bent over at waist, legs straight and hands clasped behind butt. Partner holds ball in front of his face and drops ball. Reacting man must catch it before it hits the floor.

30. DRIBBLE SUICIDE
 (i) Right hand then left hand
(ii) Change hands every turn.

31. TWO BALL DRIBBLE SUICIDE
As for 30, but use 2 basketballs.

32. CHINESE DRIBBLE SUICIDE
Out, go forwards as normal, but coming back, go backwards dribbling the ball with you. Left and right hands.

33. TWO BALL DRIBBLE AROUND BODY
Dribble 2 basketballs around legs, behind back, through legs etc.

Dribbling

An important aspect of basketball and more specifically in ball handling is dribbling. It is very important that all players learn to dribble equally well with either hand, but it is more important to know when to use the dribble. In almost all situations if a player is open ahead of the ball handler, a pass should be made rather than dribbling. There are three basic purposes of the dribble:
  1. To penetrate to the basket.
  2. To improve the passing angles to team mates.
  3. To get the ball up court against the press.

The secret to good dribbling lies in your wrists and fingertips. You must develop good control with the finger pads, and you must develop and coordinate your feet to the rhthym of the bounce. Quick hands are not enough.

Other factors to be considered in order to improve dribbling:

1. Keep the head and eyes up.
2. Do not watch the ball.
3. Keep your knees bent.
4. Maintain good body balance.
5. Spread your fingers wide.
6. Heel of your hand should be up and away with the palm on a downward slant.
7. Keep wrist firm – but not stiff.
8. Dribbling is done actually with the forearm – it is the motion of your elbow travelling through the forearm to your wrists and fingertips that provides the motion to bounce and move the ball.
9. Protect the ball with your body – put body between ball and opponent.
10. Keep your eyes on the defender/court, not the ball.
11. Watch your defender's feet to see which direction to dribble – drive towards his fron foot.
12. Keep ball low and bounce it firmly.
13. Practice with each hand.
14. Learn to change hands, speed and direction.
15. While dribbling always keep your eyes up and open for a team mate in a scoring position.

Drills

1. ZIG-ZAG DRILL
A full court dribble with a defender covering all the time – baseline to baseline. Then switch over. The dribbler must protect the dribble keeping it low. Use both hands at varying speeds, crossover dribble etc.

2. DRIBBLE TAG
Using half court and as many players as desired, one or two players are designated as 'it'. They must try and tag the other players on their back. When players are tagged they drop out. Or, when players are tagged they become 'it'.

3. DRIBBLE TAG WITH LIVES

As players are tagged they stand still with legs apart and the ball above their head. They can be made 'live' again by someone who is still alive with his dribble coming and dribbling through their legs – ball and man!

4. PARTNER DRIBBLE

In a confined area e.g. the foul circle, two players each dribbling a basketball try to knock the other's ball out of the area.

5. KING OF THE COURT

All players dribbling in say, half the court – palyers are trying to knock somebody's ball away from them. If player has ball knocked out, they drop out. As fewer players are left, Coach makes the area smaller and smaller. See which player remains with ball.

Dribble moves

1. Perform all moves with left and right hands on both sides of the court.
2. Keep head up at all times. Look up at the rim.
3. Stay low.
4. Control/feel/fingertips.
5. SPEED DRIBBLE: out in front and 'chase'. High bounce.
6. CONTROL DRIBBLE: low bounce. More to the side.
7. CROSSOVER DRIBBLE: Change from right hand to left hand (and left to right) in front of body. Low and quick.
8. HESITATION DRIBBLE: (Stutter feet) . . . stop & go.
19. SPIN DRIBBLE: Same hand. All the way round.
10. REVERSE DRIBBLE: begin to spin, but when half way round, change hands. (Practice both hands).
11. BEHIND THE BACK DRIBBLE: Use for a reason!

Drills

1. PHANTOM DRIBBLING

Coach calls out instructions, players make imaginary moves.

2. SPEED DRIBBLE LAY UP

Full court.

3. 1 ON 1 PROTECT DRIBBLE
One player with ball or both players with basketballs; try and knock ball out of pre-specified area.

4. OBSTACLE DRIBBLING
Each time the dribbler comes to an obstacle (whole length of court) he must use good footwork to go around it and must change hands using crossover dribble, behind the back dribble or reverse dribble. (Can use chairs or cones as obnstacles).

5. CHANGE OF PACE REACTION DRILL
With or without basketballs. Players amke a change of pace on the sound of Coach's whistle. Can also introduce other moves to this drill.

The following drills should begin on the right side half of the court, go in for the lay up, dribble out to left side of half court, repeat same move with left hand, then return to right side.

6. HESITATION DRIBBLE
Stop and go, lay up.

7. STUTTER DRIBBLE
Machine gun your feet, lay up.

8. SPIN DOUBLE
(i) Shoot with same hand (ii) Go under and shoot with opposite hand

9. FAKE SPIN
Keep it on same hand.

10. CROSSOVER
(i) Shoot with opposite hand (ii) Double cross-over, shoot with same hand.

11. FAKE CROSSOVER OR 'V' DRIBBLE

12. BEHIND THE BACK
Shoot with the opposite hand.

13. DRIBBLE THE FLOOR
Using all dribble moves, dribble the whole floor.

14. JAB, GO AND POWER
Jab step, drive, jump stop and shoot the power lay up.

15. DRIBBLE TO CORNER, HESITATION, HEAD & SHOULDER FAKE, REVERSE
Dribble out of the corner with right hand (right side) hitting on left foot, make reverse lay up with right hand.

16. DRIVE AND SPIN
Dribble towards end line, spin out, pull back for lay up or baby hook.

17. ACROSS FOR JUMPER
Drive across the lane for jumper.

18. ACROSS, HESITATION DRIBBLE & GO
Drive across the lane, make hesitation continue to drive for lay up.
19. ACROSS SND SPIN
Drive across lane, use spin dribble when 'cut off' and go in for lay up (right hand if driving across from left right to left,.

20. ACROSS, FAKE SPIN & GO
As for 19, except fake spin and go in for lay up (left hand if driving from right to left).

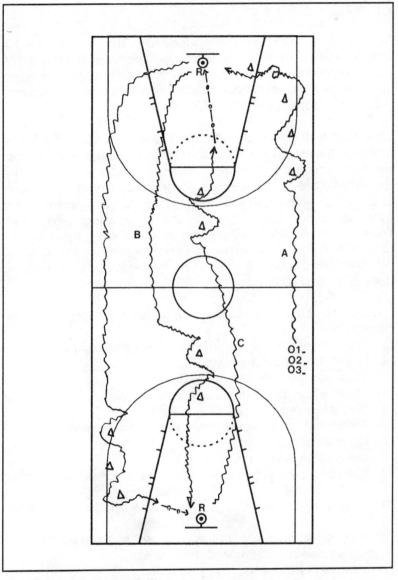

Multi Purpose Dribbling Drill.
(A) O1 performs change of pace dribble, spin and crossover dribble.
(B) After lay up & rebound, speed dribble to the chairs, perform
X-over & spin dribble, shoot.
(C) Rebound, go hard to other end, same moves at chairs, shoot collect.
(D) Dribble up sideline – use cahnge of pace dribble, same moves
round chairs, shoot – END.

Passing

Everyone who plays the game is expected to know how to pass. But without practice, there is no way you can become great at this skill. A guard who always finds the open man, who can penetrate and make things happen, who can run the offence and who makes sharp, snappy passes will be invaluable to his team.

Most basketball games are won by the team who makes the fewest mistakes. A bad pass that was made with poor judgement in a certain situation – a pass is one that was forced into traffic or a chest pass that should have been a bounce pass. Showing off is trying to do some-thing fancy in a game that you haven't practiced. More games are lost by a bad turnover than by a last second shot that went in the basket. You must work hard everyday at your passing if you are to become a great ball handler. Chances are you won't become a good passer if you have to watch the ball or turn your back when you are dribbling towards the basket.

The following fundamentals should be adhered to when developing the skill:
1. Follow through – snap the wrist throwing thumbs down.
2. Protect the ball with your body.
3. Create a good passing angle and lane.
4. Feed the post man high and look for target hand.
5. Try not to 'telegraph' your pass – fake it.
7. Keep your head up and an eye on player's movements.
6. Make sharp, snappy passes.
8. Use peripheral vision.
9. Make your pass accurate and timely so it is easy for the receiver to catch the ball.
10. Don't throw the ball just to get rid of it, have a purpose for passing.

Receiving the pass correctly is as important as throwing the pass. Points to emphasize while receiving the ball are:
1. Meet the ball and 'look' it into your hands.
2. Upon receiving a high pass, the thumbs should be together (inside).
3. Upon receiving a low pass, the thumbs should be out.
4. Protect the ball while pivoting – keep body between ball and opponent.

Drills

2 BALL 2 MAN PASSING
One player chest pass, the other players bounce pass at the same time. (Players are facing each other approx. 15' apart). Change after 1 minute. Also, one player chest pass, the other overhead pass.
Also, both players right hand only pass.
Then both players left hand only.
Also, both players behind the back right hand only.
Then both players behind the back left hand only.

MEDICINE BALL PASSING
Chest, overhead passes with a medicine ball: stationary, on the move, with sit ups etc.

15 PASS DRILL
Two teams of players (six or seven per team is OK), no shooting and no dribble except one dribble to improve the passing angle. Target is to make 15 passes in a row without the defence touching it. (Deflections count!). However, you cannot pass it to you.

2 ON 2 PASSING
Players have to make a pre-specified number of passes.

3 ON 3 PASSING
As 2 On 2.

4 ON 4 PASSING
As above.
For the above, no shooting, no dribbling, ½ court area only).

FULL COURT PASSING
2 on 2, 3 on 3, 4 on 4. (The players start at one end and attempt to get the ball to the other end without the defence touching it. Only allow passes to go ¼ court distance. Only one or two dribbles allowed. Can finish with an attempt at the basket).

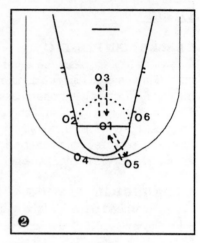

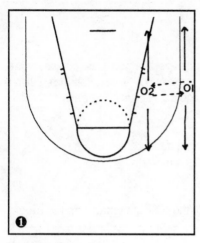

Shuffle Pass.

Both players in 'basketball stance', pass the ball to each other at irregular intervals.

Circle Pepper Pot.

Pass back to the person that passed to you. Speed it up!

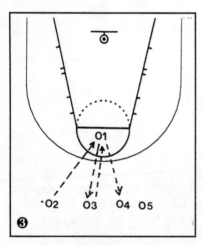

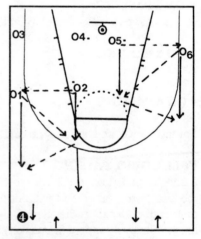

Line Pepper Drill.

Use two basketballs – pass to the next 'open' man in line. Full speed!

Full court Passing.

Players go up the court making chest passes then bounce passes. Full speed.

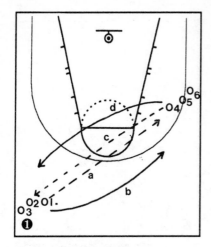

Corner Passing Drill.

Continuous. Use chest pass then bounce pass.

Also, hand-off pass.

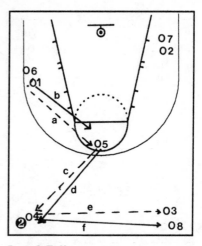

Pass & Follow.

In teams. Coach designates target number. Can pass to any spot you like, but follow the pass and fill that spot. first team to reach target wins.

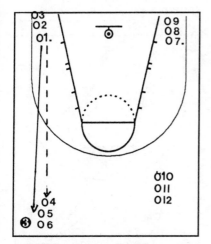

Original Positions WIN.

Pass and follow. When you arrive back at your starting spots, first team to do that, wins!

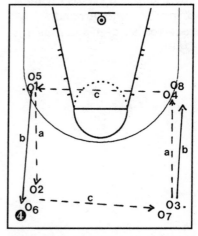

Four Corner Passing.

Begin with two basketballs. Progress to four! On Coach's whistle, change direction of pass.

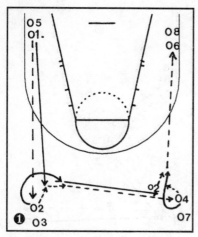

Four Corner With Hand-Off.

Start with one ball, work up to two, with change of direction on whistle. O1 pass to O2 and follow, as he approaches, O2 returns pass, O1 comes to one count stop and makes reverse pivot. O2 comes around, receives hand-off and passes to O4 etc.

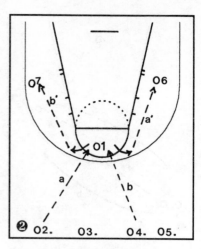

Entry Pass & Backdoor.

If pass comes from O2's side, O1 makes drop step with left foot and makes a right hand bounce pass to O6. Vice versa from other side. Increase speed.

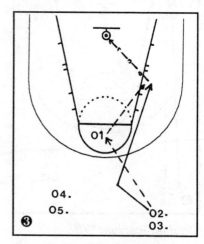

Entry Pass to High Post & Cut.

O1 will receive passes from both sides. O2 & O4 swap sides after the shot. Change O1 every minute.

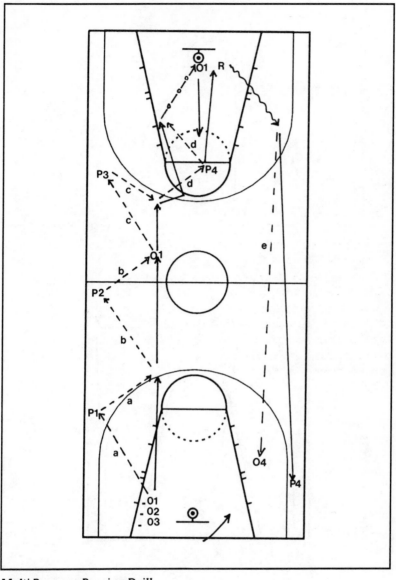

Multi Purpose Passing Drill.

(A) Chest Pass.

(B) Bounce Pass.

(C) Overhead Pass.

(D) Post Entry Pass (depends where P4 signals for it). O1 shoots, P4 rebounds. O1 replaces P4. P4 escape dribble.

(E) Baseball pass to O4. P4 follow pass & join line.

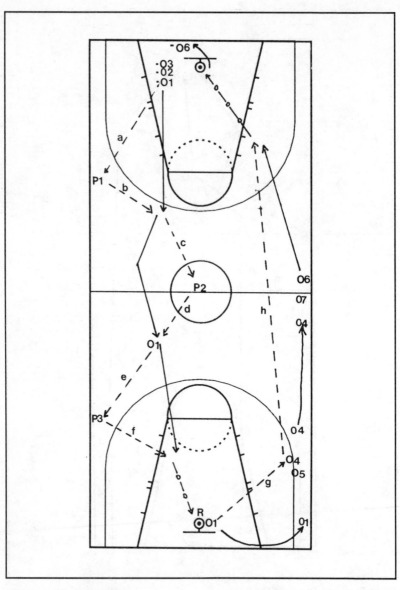

"Ball –" "Outlet Drill".

(A) P1 yells "<u>outlet</u>". O1 pass; (B) P1 pass to O1; (C) P2 yells "<u>ball</u>" O1 pass; (D) P2 passes to O1; (E) P3 yells "<u>ball</u>". O1 pass; (F) P3 pass to O1 for lay up; (G) O4 yells "<u>outlet</u>". O1 pass; (H) O6 takes off and yells "<u>ball</u>". O4 pass O6 lay up & goes to start. Rotate lines as shown.

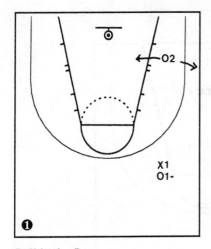

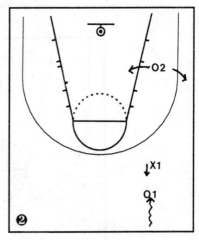

Bull in the Pen.

Defensive player must pressure the passer. O1 must try to pass to O2. Find the "gaps" e.g. near ears etc. Use fakes.

Dribble Bull in the Pen.

As previous except O1 approaches X1 on the dribble and does not pick his dribble up until the moment he is going to pass.

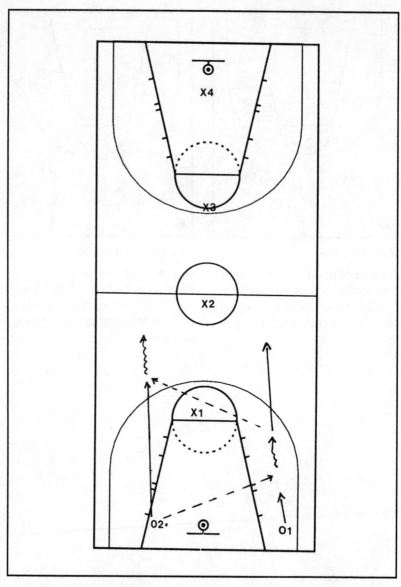

Open Lane Passing Drill.

The defenders are active and trying to deflect passes. Offensive players are to pass the ball up court, only use a dribble IF NECESSARY on 'read' of the defensive player. Try to score at this end.

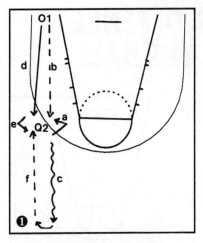 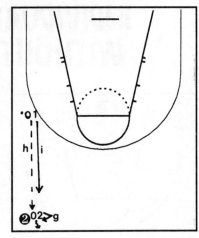

Partner Fundamentals Drill.

O1 triple threat.

(A) O2 fake away, come back, post up.

(B) O1 pass to post.

(C) O2 reverse pivot (protect ball), dribble to 10 sec. line. Jump stop, reverse pivot.

(D) O1 run to foul line.

(E) Jump stop, fake away, post up.

(F) O2 pass to O1.

(G) O2 fake, post up.

(H) O1 pass to O2. O2 reverse pivot, dribble to opposite foul line.

(I) O1 run and jump stop at 10 sec. line.

Repeat all the way up & back.

INDIVIDUAL OFFENCE WITHOUT THE BALL

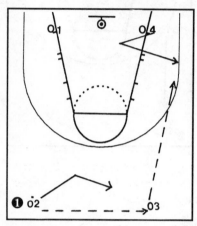

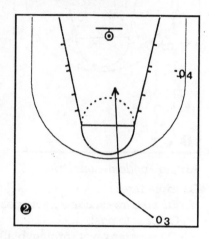

3 Man Drills.

L cuts and V cuts, passing, triple threat position etc. Perform first with no defence and simply rotate as shown above. Then add defence on all players.

If the forward (on the wing) is not open at any time then make the guard pass and try and enter on the other side.

O2 pass to O3. O2 & O4 V cut as shown. O3 pass to O4 & O3 V cut to basket.

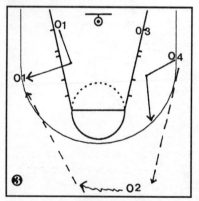

O4 pass to O2. O1 V cut & receive pass from O2 (who has made a good angle for this pass by use of dribble). O4 V cut to top of lane. O2 V cut to basket. Repeat

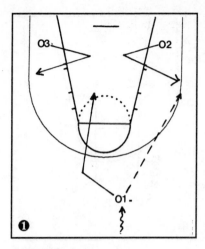

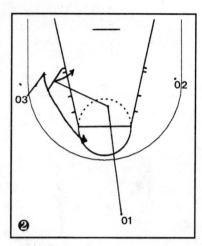

3 Man Motion.

Pass & cut to basket. Give and Go.

Pass and screen away. Can hit O3 for foul line jumper or O1 on roll to basket.

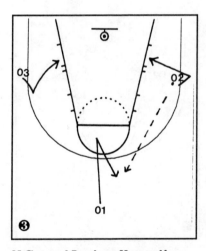

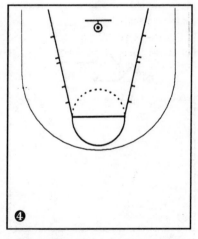

V Cut and Replace Yourself.

Wings go backdoor. Can hit either wing man for lay up or O1 can shoot the Jump shot.

In all drills, all 3 men are active. The non-shooters are crashing boards for the rebound.

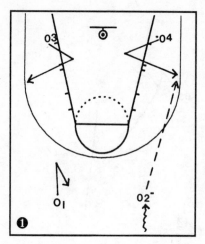

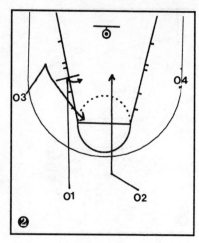

Four on Four. Offensive Shell Drill.
Cuts etc. as shown. Keep 15'–18' spacing at all times. Options vary,
but ones shown are the obvious and simplest ones,
Can add defence later.

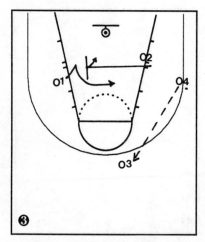

O1, O3, O4 all V cut to get open. O2 pass to O4. O2 cut to basket
(for give & go option). O1 screen down for O3. O4 pass to O3 who
has popped out. O2 lateral screen for O1. O1 back screen for O4.
O3 pass to O4 for backdoor lay up.

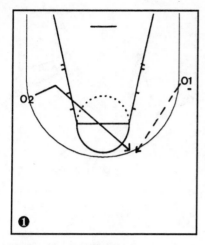

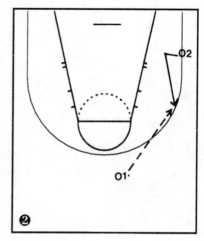

Cut to the Ball Drills.

Cut hard to an area in scoring range. Catch the ball. Face the basket (triple threat).

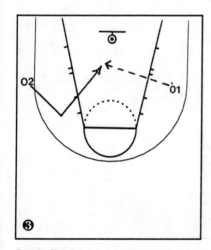

Back Cuts.

"Read the defence". Perform 1 on O first, then add defensive player, but restrict play to the areas shown.

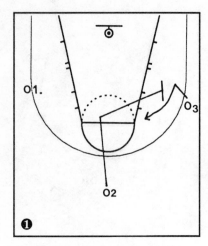

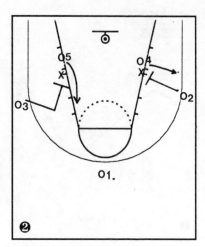

Cuts off the Screen.

Practice various cuts without defence. Above shows 'over the top' cut.

Cut around screen and up inside.

If defender is high up on the screen, back-cut off the screen.

If defender follows – curl off the screen.

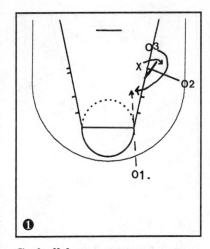

❶

Curl off the screen.

❷

If defender goes to anticipate
(behind screen) – run a flare.

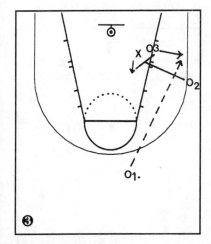

❸

Flare out off the screen.

❹

Cuts after The Screen.

If O3 curls or back cuts off the
screen, O2 will reverse pivot
towards the *mid-court* line and
the half line and step back for
ball.

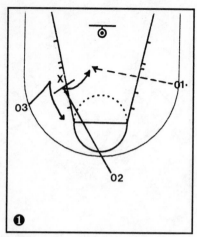

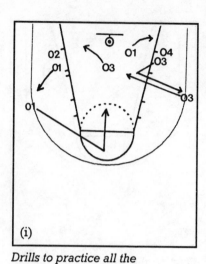

❶

If O3 goes over the top or flares off screen, O2 will Reverse pivot toward the baseline and step towards the ball.

(i)

Drills to practice all the possibilities described.
(i) 2 lines of players on either side at low post. O1 break out to wing then L cut to basket. At the same time, O3 is V cutting to wing & then back cutting to basket. They then change lines.

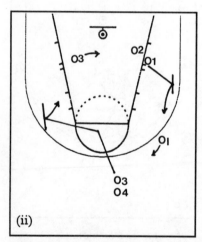

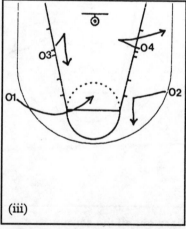

(ii)

(ii) 2 lines of players, at point & at low post. O3 screen away & roll to basket. O1 back screen & flare out. Change lines.

(iii)

(iii) 4 lines. Low post both sides & free throw line extended both sides. O1 curl cut (or C cut) to basket. O2 L cut & flare out. O3 V cut & duck in. O4 V cut & break out.

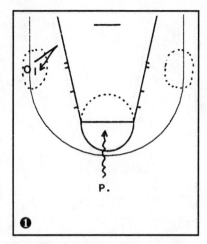

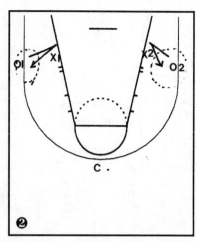

Spot UP-Get Open. O1 can only shoot from specified areas. Must get open continuously. P can dribble-drive and dish it.

2 on 2. Coach passes ball to wing. First wing man to get it can dribble, the other cannot. O2 can only dribble three times but he can only shoot from specified areas (after pass). O1 is getting open in any shooting area. O2 is looking to drive, draw & dish. Coach may be used to reverse the ball.

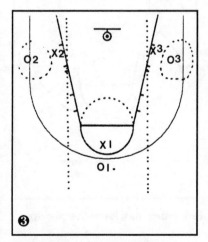

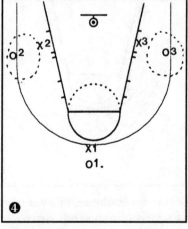

3 on 3. O1 can do what he wants, but only in specifed 'corridor'. O2 & O3 can only shoot from specified areas.

Live, but only O3 can dribble (3) & O2 cannot. (O1 can do what he likes). Then O2 & O3 switch roles. Make & take up to 5, then Xs get ball.

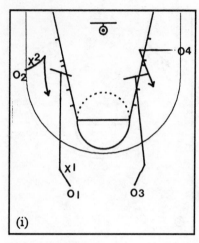

(i)

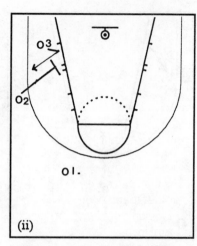

(ii)

Use of Screens
2 on 2 Downscreen. Read the defence. O2 can pop up to high post, can curl, can cut backdoor (duck in) or can fade.

Combo lateral & up Screen. (ii)–(iv): O2 lateral screen for O3 who pops out. O1 pass to O3 on wing. O2 up-screen for O1 who makes UCLA cut. O3 pass to O2 & repeat.

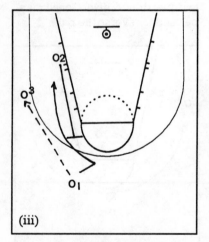

(iii)

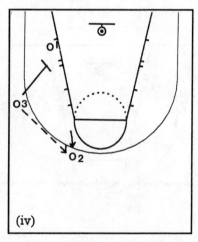

(iv)

Ensure all fundamentals are executed. Later, can have the player using the screen shoot/drive.

REBOUNDING

1. There is nothing fancy about rebounding. It requires great determination. Don't be afraid to get hit by an opponent.
2. Just think that you own a piece of property under the basket that you don't want to give to anyone, especially someone from the other team.
3. Blocking out has to be habitual, something you want to do – a natural instinct for you.
4. You must check off your man for about 1–2 seconds. Know when to move or jump for the loose ball.
5. Everytime the ball is shot, find someone to box out.
6. Rebound using angles to find your man. If you know where the ball is it is easier to position yourself with the proper angle to rebound.
7. Jumping is very important in rebounding but also is the most tiring movement in the game. Go up high and strong, land with a big base to the floor and look quickly for an outlet pass.
8. Pivot to the outside for an outlet pass. Use escape dribble if necessary.
9. Perform jumping drills everyday, e.g. jump 100 times as high as you can; touch ring or backboard 20 times with each hand.
10. A rebound is a loose ball – whoever wants it can get it.

4 Principles for Effective Rebounding

1. Positioning.
2. Capturing the rebound.
3. Protecting the rebound.
4. The outlet pass.

1. POSITIONING
Keep the opponent on your back. Know where your man is when the shot is taken. Use a pivot to block him out before he moves for the rebound. Be aggressive and quick thinking with the position you take. On a mismatch situation only concern yourself with denying the ball from the person you are guarding. A front pivot can be an advantage.

2. CAPTURING THE REBOUND

Using timing, leg spring, body and hand control, coil your body upwards and with an angle to the basket. Snap the ball out of the air with both hands. Keep elbows out and feet spread. Grip the ball firmly with both hannds. Turn in the air towards the side you will outlet the ball to. Land with broad base on balance, knees bent in a power position.

3. PROTECTING THE REBOUND

Bring the ball down to the chest area (no lower) with elbows out. Knees bent and trunk slightly bent over the ball. Look for outlet to the sideline.

4. THE OUTLET

Use two hands to outlet pass the ball. Use fakes, pivots if necessary.

Drills

1. JUMP ROPE

Use as many different 'moves' as possible.

2. VERTICAL JUMPS

To touch rim or backboard. Keep hands up throughout.

3. RUN THE STEPS

At your arena etc.

Butt to Butt Drill

Two players are stationed in one of the three circles on the court. Their backs are arched against each other. They have a wide base, arms are up in the air fully extended. Upon the Coach's whistle, each player drives for the other with the buttock's, back legs and tries to force him out of the circle. Players must maintain a good body balance and yet push without the use of the arms.

Meatgrinder or "The Pit"

For this drill put any number of players in the lane and tell them that they can get out of The Pit by grabbing and outletting TWO rebounds. The Coach shoots the ball and the players go after it. No pushing with hands. Arms have to be up in the air.

This may be adapted as an offensive rebounding drill by having the players not only rebound the ball but powering it back up for the score. Two gets you out!

Super 11

1. *Rebound both sides of the board*: ("Superman Drill"). 10 each side.
2. *Tipping right/left*: Tip it 10 times and then tip it in.
3. *Race and tip*: Player aligns himself just outside the lane above the second hash mark. He tosses the ball off the board and races to tip it in. Grabs the ball, runs to other side and repeat. 5 on each side.
4. *Rip and power*: Player tosses ball up, RIPS it down with spread eagle form, regain balance and power it in. 10 each side.
5. *Rip, fake and power*: As for 4 except when player comes back down, he gives a good head-pump fake and then powers. 10 each side.
6. *Rip, step under*: Player throws ball off board. Comes down. Steps underneath to the other side of the hoop and reverses it in.
7. *Rip, fake, step under*: Same as for 6, but add a fake before stepping under.
8. *Rip and hook*: Throw ball off board, rip it down, and make baby hook in the middle.
9. *Hand Toughner*: Throw ball off board, grab it above the rim hit ball against the rim as you come down with it. (For the bigger players!).
10. *Two ball dunks*: Coach places two balls on the low blocks. Player picks ball up and dunks as many as he can whilst alternating sides.
11. *Super Slam*: Player starts at 3rd free throw hash mark extended, tosses ball off board at an angle that will carom it over front of rim. He races into the middle and slam dunks it. Smaller players can tip it in. 5–10 reps., both sides.

Superman with Offence

This drill is similar to the Superman Drill, except on rebounding the ball outside of the lane, player will execute a back to the basket move.

After a while introduce a defender who may come in once the ball has been rebounded.

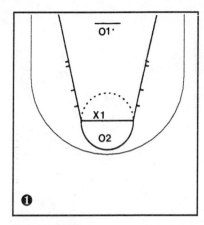

❶

Pointer Drill.

O1 has the ball. X1 has his back to O1. O2 reacts in the direction that O1 points the ball, X1 makes pivot and blocks out O2.

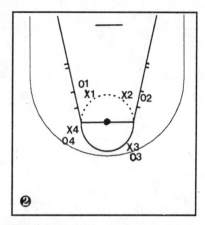

❸

Superman Drill.

Player throws ball against board, high and on the other side of the rim. Takes one step, jumps and catches ball at top of his jump, trying to land on the other side of the paint. Go side to side for one minute. Two hands on the ball.

❷

Circle Rebounding.

Player's line up as shown. On Coach's whistle the offensive players try to get into the circle to grab the ball. On the second whistle the drill stops. (About 1½ secs. in between). Defensive players must try to block out legally. Elbows up.

❹

Rebound & Outlet Drill.

Coach shoots. Two players contest (X1 & O1) rebound. If defender gets it he makes outlet pass. If O1 gets it – it's 1 on 1.

73

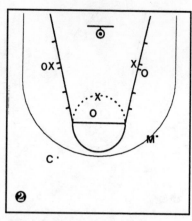

❶

As previous except it's now 2 on 2. Progress to 3 on 3 then 4 on 4.

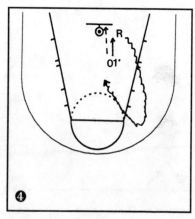

❷

Angle Rebound Drill.

Coach shoots ball. Defence must block out and rebound. If offence get it, defence do push ups. Defence need 3 rebounds IN A ROW to come out. The defensive rebound must be outletted to where it was shot from. If the pass is stolen…rebound doesn't count!

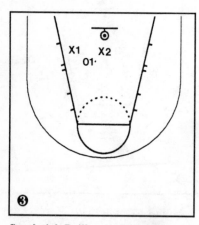

❸

Sandwich Drill.

Three players are lined up in front of the basket. The middle man tosses the ball up for himself. He tries to rebound it and go right back up for the score. The Xs muscle him, 'foul' him etc.

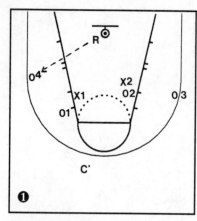

❹

Rebound & Wheel.

O1 throws ball up, rebounds it and in one motion turns to sideline whilst keeping ball high. He pump fakes the pass & dribbles out and back to other side of rim – repeat.

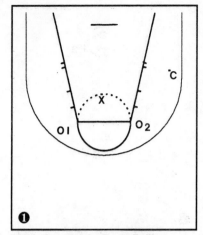

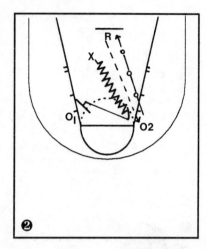

Block Out, Hustle, React Drill.
Coach shoots, he calls out either 1 or 2. That player must go for the rebound (in this example it was O1). X blocks him out and gets rebound. X makes good pass to the other offensive player who shoots a jump shot as X goes to close out on him. Meanwhile the non-shooter has moved back to his starting spot; as soon as the shot is up this player goes to the boards again and X must hustle over and box him out. If coach yells "get it" – all three men crash the boards.

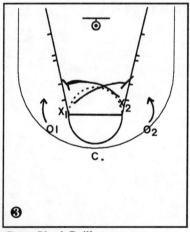

Cross Block Drill.
Coach shoots, defenders must cross the lane, find the offensive rebounder and box him out. If defenders get it they outlet it to Coach. If offensive get it – it"s 2 on 2.

75

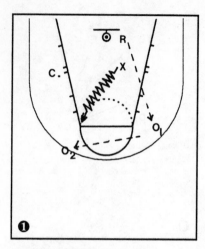

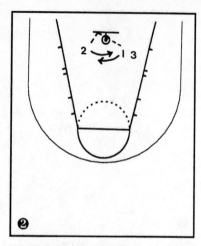

Multi Purpose Rebound.

Coach puts ball off glass. X rebounds it, outlet to O1. O1 pass to O2 who shoots. X must hustle to close out on shot. O2 goes for rebound, X block out & compete for rebound. If X gets it he outlets to Coach, if O2 gets it, it's 1 on 1.

UCLA Anti-Over Drill.

1 puts ball up high and over rim. Moves to 2's side, 2 is tipping it back to the other side for 3. 2 goes to opposite side, 3 tips to 1 and moves, etc. 1 minute.

FAST BREAK

1. Fill the lanes – get up the floor QUICKLY.
2. Look ahead – see the whole floor. See options. If a team mate is ahead of you and is open – give him the ball.
3. See what the defence is doing – make decisions and execute accordingly.
4. make good cuts.
5. Pass the ball up the floor rather than dribbling – if possible.
6. Establish a philosophy and pattern which you as a Coach prefer. (There are various types of fast break including the sideline break).
7. Drill with a purpose.

The fast break begins with a defensive block out, a defensive rebound and an outlet pass – these should be drilled and taught first and should always be emphasized in the fast break drills. The drills outlined here are for the PRIMARY fast break.

1 FULL SPEED
Three on zero fast break. The three players must make four layups (ie. up and back twice) in 20 seconds without the ball touching the floor.

2 TRANSITION DRILL
Two teams play 5 on 5 fast breaking on every possession. Dribbling limited by Coach. On the Coach's whistle, whoever has the ball at the moment simply puts it down still on the floor. The other team must grab the ball real quick and filling the lanes, fast break toward their opponent's basket.

Teaches quick and rapid transition from defence to offence and also from offence to defence. Also teaches keeping heads up and seeing early pass opportunities; filling the lanes quickly and of course is a great conditioner!

Keep the score – play to e.g. 7.

3 TRANSITION-CONDITIONER

Play live 5 on 5 e.g. Blue vs white. If blues make the shot, all the play-ers must sprint back and put a foot in the paint before being able to defend against the oncoming white team. If blues miss the shot, all players must touch the baseline before being able to defend. Play to say, 8 baskets.

4 THE 7 SECOND SHOT CLOCK

Play live 5 on 5, if you score you get the ball out of the net, inbound it and go. You must attempt a (decent)! shot within 7 seconds or you lose the ball and the other team get it in the half court and run one of your half court offensive plays. Play to say, 8 baskets.

5 FIRST SEVEN OR LAST TEN

Play live 5 on 5 full court. You must score within the first 7 seconds of the shot clock or during the last 10 seconds of the shot clock!

(During the 7–20 second period if you have an open lay up then you can score it). Coach needs to audible signals (apart from his whistle) to make players aware of the end of 7 secs. and beginning of last 10 secs.

6 LAKERS FAST BREAK

Play life 5 on 5 full court. If you score you take ball out of net, inbound and go the other way. Play to say, 8 baskets.

7 LOOK & PASS AHEAD

Start in half court, 3 on 3 with the Coach throwing ball off backboard. If defence get it they fast break to other end NO DRIBBLE in the back-court. Teams then go end to end like this for e.g. 5 trips. Keep score.

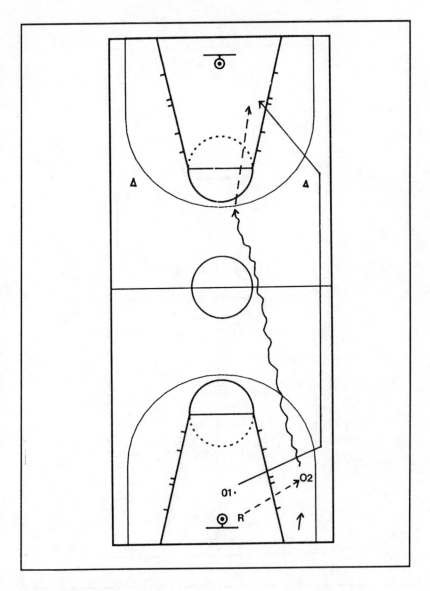

2 Man Fast Break.

Shoot lay ups first, both sides, then jump shots. O1 steps out and tosses ball up on backboard, rebounds it & makes outlet pass to O2 who yells "outlet!". O2 speed dribble to other end. O1 Fill the lane and run outside of the cone. O2 jump stop under control, pass to O1 who lays it up, O2 rebound the ball. Repeat coming back down the other side. (O1 goes to the outlet spot).

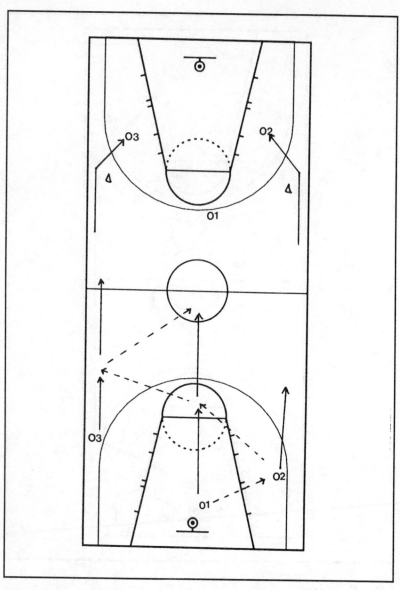

3 Man Interpass Drill.

Only dribble if you are going to commit travel violation.

Can run the drill up and back or one way only.

Or all three must make a lay up. Ball must not touch floor.

Can put a 'time' on it i.e. 4 secs to score ...

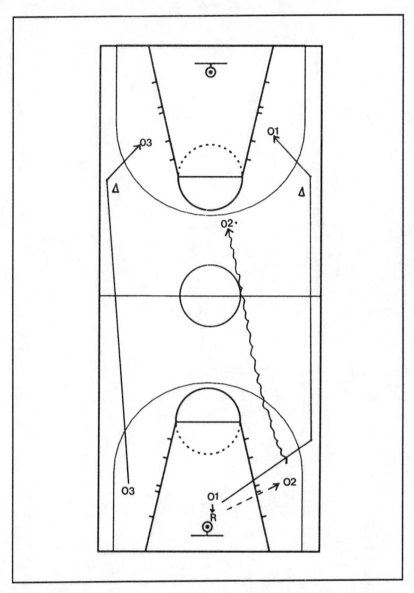

3 on 0 Outlet Fast Break.

Can add defence to all these drills. At the rebound end, in the
middle of the floor, and at the shooting end.

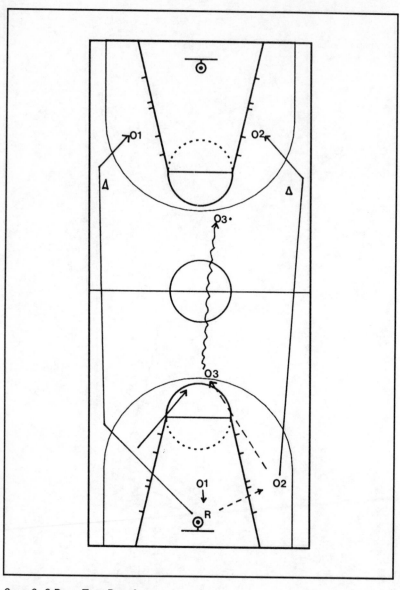

3 on 0, 2 Pass Fast Break.

Take lay ups first, then bank shots, then "automatic" shot. i.e. O3 will pass to e.g. O2, O2 will get into triple threat. O3 will fake away and cut back to ball receive it at the 'elbow' and shoot the jumper or hit O1 or O3 who have cut 'backdoor'. Non-shooters will rebound.

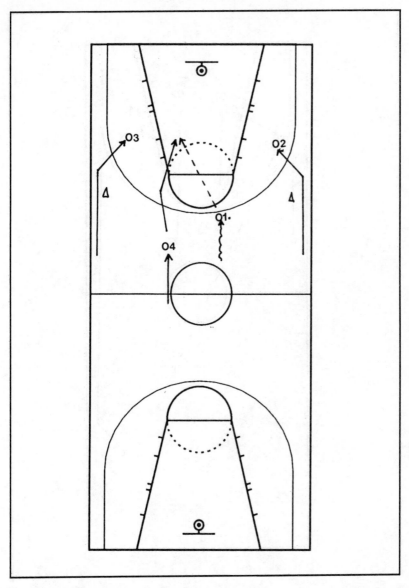

4 Man Fast Break.

As previous drills, except introduce a trailer.

Start drill by Coach shooting and all four players go for rebound. Rebounder is the trailer.

Can execute any option to score including pass to trailer.

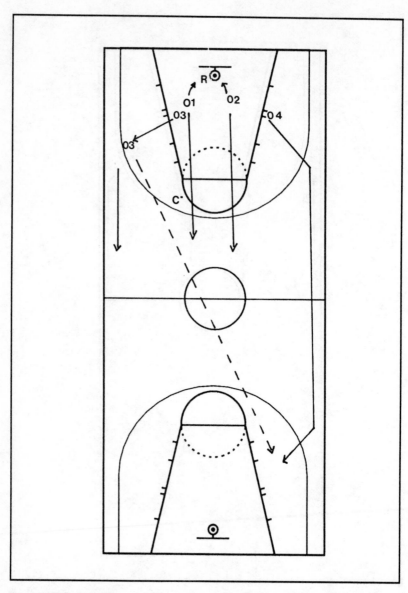

Baseball Pass Drill.

Coach shoots. Players compete for rebound. Pass etc. as shown. All players trail the break & tip in or rebound, or inbound the ball at the other end and repeat drill coming the other way.

In this diagram, O1 secured the rebound, outlet passed to O3, O4 broke down court.

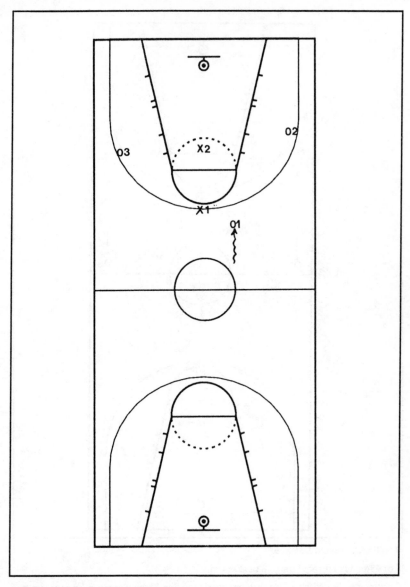

3 on 2, 2 on 1. Or, 4 on 2, 2 on 2.

Players come up the floor as per other drills versus 2 defenders. The player who shoots or touches it last comes back on defence versus X1 & X2.

For 4 on 2, 2 on 2 ... players must talk to get a second player back.

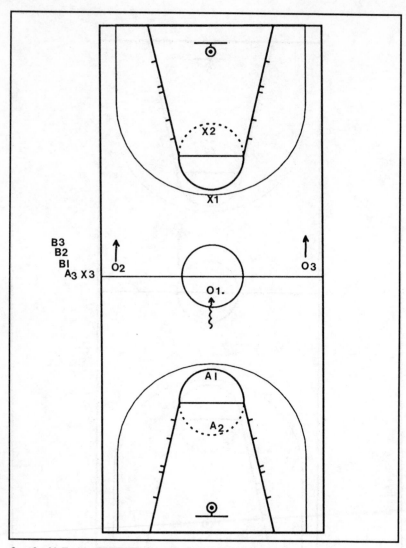

3 on 2 with Trailing Defence.

3 or 4 teams of three. First to 8 baskets wins.

Os attack vs Xs. When all Os have crossed time line X3 may come in by running, put one foot in centre circle and join his teammates.

Os vs Xs till Os score or Xs get ball.

Xs will attack the other end, & Os will play tough defence back to the half.

Xs vs As.

Bs will move in at the other end.

Continues till target is reached.

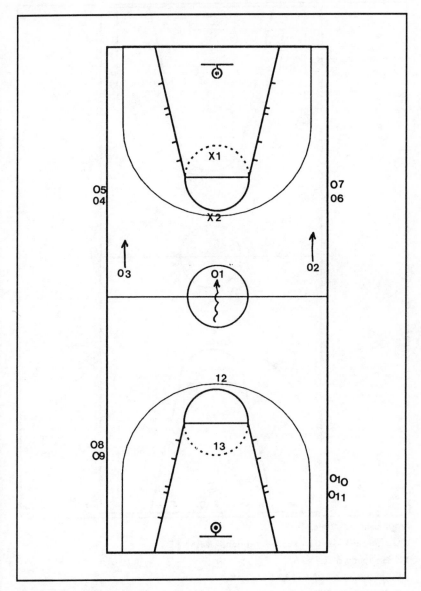

11 Man Fast Break Drill.

It is a 3 on 2 drill. Whoever wins the rebound (only one shot attempt), at each end, outlets to the strongside and they break to the other end along with the weakside outlet man.

See which player can "stay in the drill" the longest.

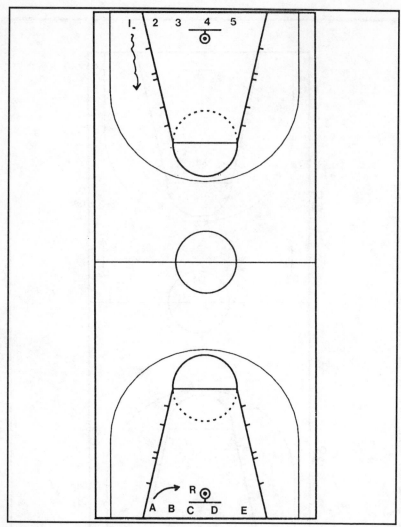

Progressive Fast Break Drill.

No. 1 goes FC 1 on 0 for score A rebounds & A vs 1 FC.

1 & 2 rebound & 1&2 vs A.

B & A rebound & B&A vs 1&2.

1, 2, 3 vs A, B. A, B, C, vs 1, 2, 3.

1, 2, 3, 4 vs A, B, C.

A, B, C, D vs 1, 2, 3, 4.

1, 2, 3, 4, 5 vs A, B, C, D.

5 on 5.

END.

Repeat with A starting the drill 1 on 0.

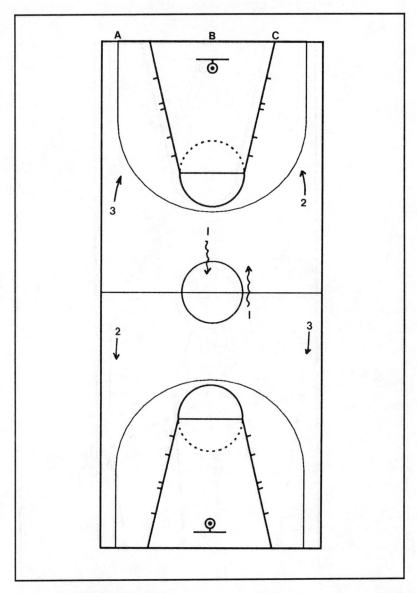

Continuous 3 Man Fast Break.

1, 2, 3 go up and back as for normal 3 man break.

Outlet man must yell "ball" or "outlet", middle man must yell "ball" or "middle".

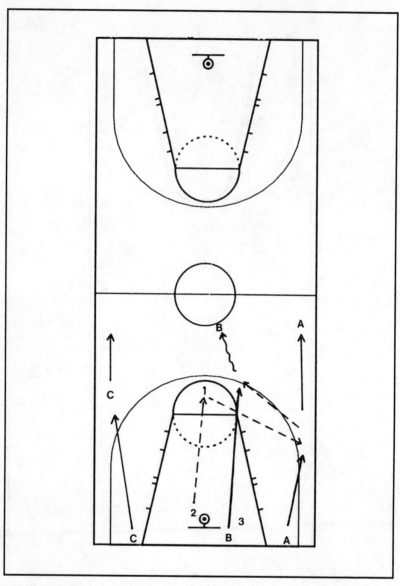

Continuous 3 Man Fast Break (continued).

Non shooter (2) rebounds and outlets the ball to 1. 1 outlets to A and in the meantime B has made a sprint-cut up the middle to get pass from A. Drill thus continues in this way.

DEFENCE

1 STANCE
Feet (heel-toe)
legs
butt
back
head
eyes.

2 HANDS
Up, out in front, active.

3 SLIDE
Lead and drag, step and slide. Keep feet spread. Don't cross feet. Stay low.

4 REACTION
Quickly. Be ready and alert – always.

5 PERIPHERAL VISION
See your man and the ball together at all times.

6 PRESSURE
Relentlessly, all the time.

7 BLOCKING OUT
All players must. Make contact. Watch flight of the ball from shot first, offensive player's movement next, and then go for rebound angle.

8 DENIAL DEFENCE
Defence versus man without the ball – one pass away . . . deny. 'Open' up OR 'snap head' if your man goes backdoor. Front or bump cutters.

9 DEFENCE VERSUS MAN WITH BALL
When dribble has been used up – "Belly up and pressure".
When dribble is 'live', be one arm's length away.
Versus a good dribbler/driver – don't get too close.
Versus a good shooter – hand up and get closer.
'Nose on the ball' versus the dribble.

Drills

MASS REACTION DRILL

1   Players are down in good defensive stance, facing the Coach. Coach signals with voice and hands. Players react. (Coach makes hand signals from his abdomen region).

Slide right   = two quick slides.

  ,,   left   = ,,   ,,   ,,

  ,,   forward = ,,   ,,   ,,

  ,,   backward = ,,   ,,   ,,

Fist with right hand – players will yell "Pick left", feel for imaginary screen, and make an 'over the top' motion with left leg, then recover. (Vice versa for left fist).

Coach yells "Left!" – players make a 180 degree turn to the left and back – fast.

Coach yells "Right!" – players make a 180 degree turn to the right and back – fast.

Coach yells "Shot!" – players yell "Shot!" and make a close out with hand up, then box out the imaginary shooter.

Coach yells "Rebound!" – players go up and grab imaginary rebound with 2 hands, land, keep "ball" under chin ("Chin it and rip it"), pivot to the outside and make imaginary outlet pass.

Coach puts hand straight up in air – players perform 'Foot Fire'.

2   Players are facing the Coach in rows, in good defensive stance. Coach will point forwards, backwards, left, right – players react by making two quick slides in that direction. Stay low, feet spread, hands up.

Coach could also have a ball, if he starts to dribble it players will shadow the dribble direction and yell "Ball, ball!" Coach puts ball above his head – players yell "Dead, dead!" and 'belly up' on ball. (Mirror the ball or trace it with both hands as Coach moves it around).

FOOT FIRE or MACHINE GUN or ALABAMA SHUFFLE DRILL

Players stutter their feet rapidly in place. On the whistle, jump around (¼ turn) and back and continue.

FOOT FIRE AND JAB

As above, but on the whistle jab with right foot and 'dig' in with right hand (as if to deflect/steal ball). On next whistle perform with left leg and hand. Yell "ball" whilst jabbing; do it quickly and resume foot fire.

FIG. 8 SHUFFLE

Use the lines of the court i.e. along baseline up sideline, across mid court line, up sideline, along opposite baseline etc. in a fig. 8 pattern. Stay low, hands and heads up, don't bring heels together.

CHINESE BOXING DRILL

2 players facing each other in defensive stance – try to slap each other's knees with their hands, whilst staying low throughout.

1 ON 1

Emphasis on defence. Play ½ court and full court. First, with the defensive player checking ball to the offensive player; then with offensive player receiving pass from a Coach, therefore defensive player has to play defence against the cut and the entry pass as well as against the dribble etc.

CLOSE OUT DRILL (Also a shooting drill)

Pass ball out to your partner from under the basket; run out a few steps then as you approach the shooter, slide with inside hand and foot up, close out on the shot and yell "Shot!". Box out then rebound. 5 and rotate.

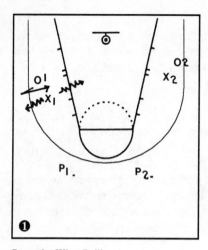

①

Deny the Wing Drill.

X1 & X2 try to prevent O1 & O2 from receiving the ball. Both hands are up. Concentrate on footwork and "flat triangle". Philosophy about backdoor cut . . . snap head or open to the ball? If O1 gets it, then go 1 on 1.

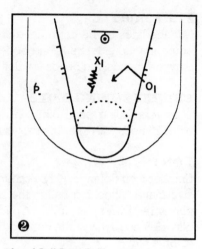

②

1 on 1 Ball Away Drill.

X1 must deny the cutter. NB. Footwork, hands, vision. Philosophy Re. "ride the man down the lane"? If O1 gets it, play 1 on 1.

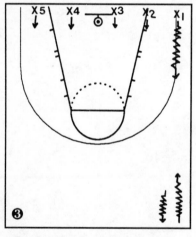

③

Forward & Backward Sliding Drill.

Players step-slide 3 to the left, drop step (or swing step) then 3 to the right backwards to mid court. Come back sliding forwards. Then go sideways slide. Hands are UP at all times.

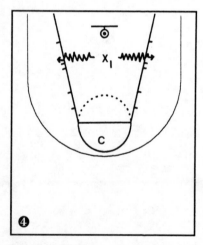

④

Make It Hurt Drill.

Player stands in good defensive stance – see how many time he can touch left & right lines in 30 seconds.

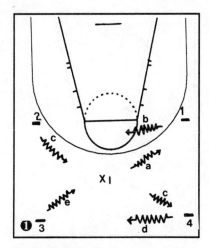

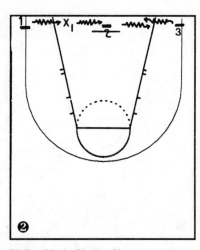

Sliding Blocks Drill.

(Use small wooden blocks). X1 has one block in his hand to start.
(a) Slides to 1, puts his block down & picks up No. 1 block.
(b) Slides horizontally picks up No. 2 block & leave No. 1. etc.
Go for 30 secs. or 1 minute. Hands are UP at all times. Feet spread. Stay down.

Sliding Blocks Along a Line.

Pick up and replace blocks as before, but at each point perform reverse pivot and continue sliding.

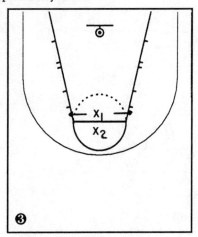

Heave Drill.

2 players either side of a line. X1 has his back to X2. X2 has his hands on X1s back. They are both in defensive stance X2 has to try to mirror X1's movement as he slides side to side whilst trying to "push" him 'off course'.

95

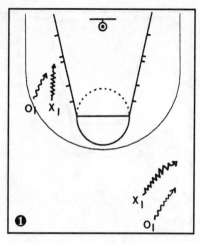

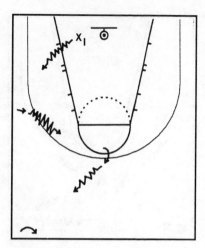

Shut the Door on the Dribble.

O1 dribbles hard towards the base-line, or sideline. X1 slides and tries to place his lead foot on (or over) the line before O1 gets there.

Angle Slides.

Begin facing the baseline. Player slides as shown, performing pivots (or swing step) at sideline and mid-court locations. Go full court.

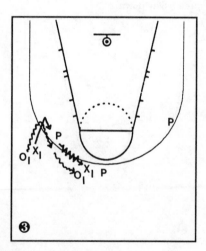

Force Over the Pick Drill.

1. No offensive player. X1 will slide to his left (then back again). When he hits a pick/screen, he should swing his lead leg out and around the pick whilst straightening up slightly to "get over the top".
2. O1 now dribbles, attempting to drive X1 into each pick. Once they get past the last pick – they go 1 on 1.

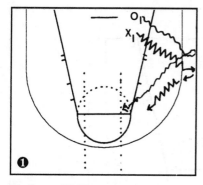

①

Zig-Zag or Z Drill.

X1 must slide (nose on ball & one arm's length) and "get to the line first", thus making O1 reverse his dribble. (Or take the charge!) If O1 can go past he does. X1 must make O1 reverse and go the opposite way. Progresss: 1. No hands. 2. O1 not allowed to go past. 3. O1 can go past. 4. Every few seconds, pick up dribble – X1 must 'belly-up', yell "Dead". 5. Z to 10 sec. line, then 1 on 1 to hoop.

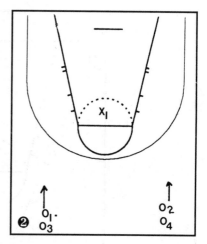

②

2 on 1.

Try to force the outside shot. Defensive man must get it twice to come out.

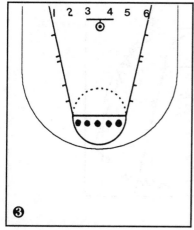

③

Toughness Drill.

Place 5 basketballs on the foul line and six players on the baseline. On the whistle, players dive for the balls. Continue, 4 balls–5 players, 3 balls–4 players etc. Find the "Team Toughie!"

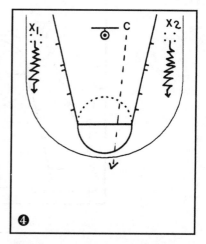

④

Heart Drill, or Who Wants It More? Drill.

Two players come out and face the baseline while backward sliding. Coach rolls or throws ball out, players go after it and go 1 on 1 at this end. Score. Whoever gets it out of the net is going on offence 1 on 1 full court to the other end.

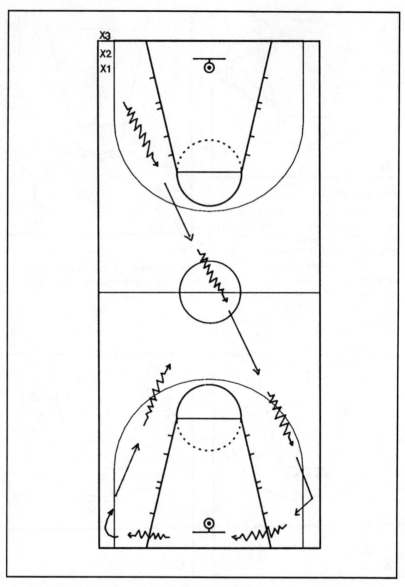

Shuffle & Chase Drill.

Players slide for 3 or 4 slides then sprint 3 or 4 paces. (Across diagonal). Then slide the base-line.

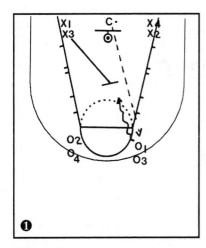

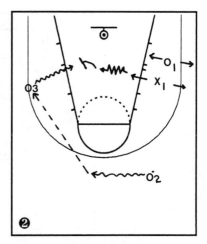

①

Take the Charge Drill.

Whichever line Coach passes to, the opposite defensive man steps out, offensive player drives to basket if lane is open. X tries to take the charge!

②

Helpside Take the Charge Drill.

X1 denies the wing pass. O2 dribbles over and passes to O3. X1 makes correct slide in relation to position of ball. O3 must drive, X1 try to take the charge.

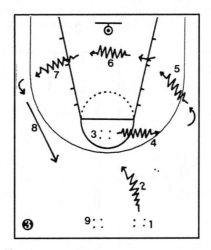

③

6 Point Defensive Drill.

1. Machine gun for 10. 2. Backward sliding. 3. Machine gun (10). 4. Sideways slide, touch line with hands. 5. Denial slide back to block. 6. Open up & lateral slide across lane. 7. Denial slide to sideline, touch with hands. 8. Jog back to half. 9. Machine gun (10), go again the other side.

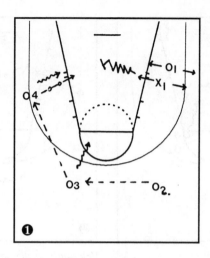

Multi Purpose Drill.

If O1 gets open, O2 pass him the ball. Go 1 on 1 with X1. If X1 denies O1 the ball, O2 passes to O3 who can drive. X1 must take the charge. O3 can pass to O4 who can drive or shoot. If he drives, X1 takes the charge. If he shoots, O1 goes for rebound and X1 must box him out. Progress: 1. When ball is with O3 or O4 they can drive & dish to O1, who must shoot. X1 must close out on the shot and then box out & rebound. 2. Coach is under the basket with a ball, after X1 has outletted the ball to O2 or O3, Coach rolls ball out and X1 must dive on it. Or, Coach lobs ball near to sideline, X1 must go after it and save it from going out of bounds.

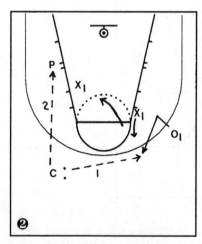 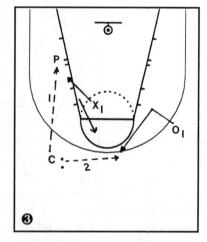

Hustle Drill. Get a deflection drill.

Coach has two basketballs. X1 must first try to deflect pass to O1, then quickly try to get the next pass into the post. Or, if post catches it, then 'help out on post'. Drill can work the other way too. i.e. First pass is into the post.

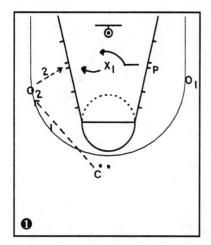 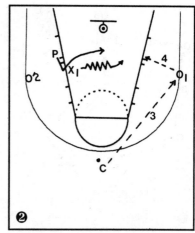

Hustle Deflection Drill in the Paint.

This drill is similar to the previous ones only now the action is from the perimeter into the post area. X1 must try to deflect/intercept two passes into the post.

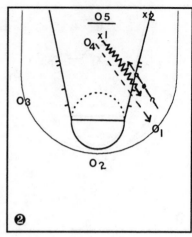
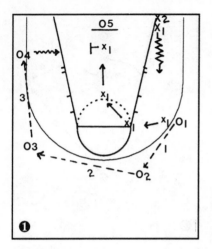

"Get Up" Drill.

X1 runs out then closes out on O1. Yell "Ball". O1 passes to O2, X1 adjusts his
position accordingly and yells "Help Left". O2 passes to O3. X1 adjusts, and yells
"help in the lane". etc. O3 pass to O4. X1 adjust. O4 drives, X1 takes the charge.
Falls over. O5 yells "get up, get up". O4 rebounds and outlets to O1, X1 rushes out
to close out on O1's jumper, X1 boxes out and gets rebound.

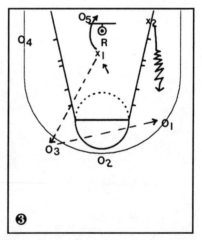

X1 outlets to O3 who calls "outlet". O3
passes to O1 and X2 comes out at this
point to repeat drill.

HELPSIDE DEFENCE
(An introduction)

1   Ball-you-man relationship at all times.
2   Ball-you-basket relationship at all times. [Flat triangle]
3   One pass away – deny.
4   One pass away – one step off passing lane, one step off man.
    Two passes away – one step off passing lane, two steps off man.
    Three passes away – one step off passing lane, three steps off man.
    ["Off the line (of ball) and up the line"]
5   Point to the man and the ball – PISTOLS.
6   Stay low, knees bent.
7   React quickly.
8   Help then recover.
9   Talk – "ball", "help", "pick left" etc.
10 Hands up – all the time.
11 Peripheral vision – very important.
12 Jump in the direction of the ball/pass.
13 Deny – 'bump' cutters.
14 SITUATIONS versus driver (baseline & top side).
                         entry pass into post.
                         flash post or cutter.
                         screen away from ball (covering).
                         on the ball screen (hedging).
15 Switching . . . a philosophy.

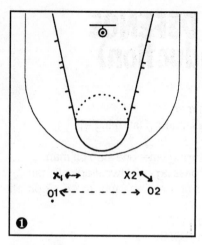

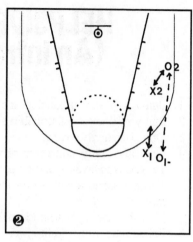

2 on 2. Indiana Drill.

Passes are made guard to guard. Man on ball yells "Ball", man off ball yells "Help left" or "Help right".

2 on 2.

Passes are made guard to forward.

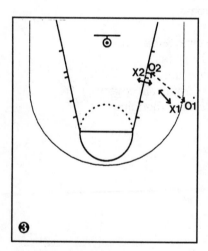

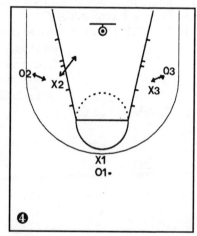

2 on 2. Forward to post.

Progressions: Add penetrating dribble. Then go 'live'.

3 on 3.

Ball moves on Coach's command. Talk, hands up, pistols, establish helpside position, react, jump to ball, footwork.

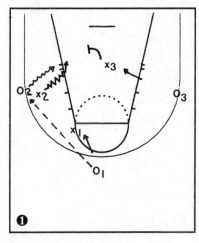

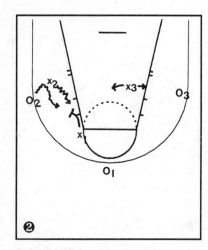

Defend the Driver.

1. Baseline: X3 must help & recover back to his man QUICKLY.

Defend the Driver.

2. Top side: X1 must help n' recover.

Each time O2 or O3 get ball they must drive hard to hoop, back the dribble out and reverse ball via O1 at the point.

Progressions: O2 & O3 can go either way.

3 on 3 live action but can only score off a drive to hoop.

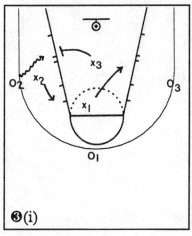

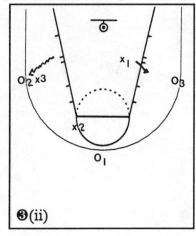

❸(i)

❸(ii)

3 on 3 Rotation.

As previous drills, but now defenders must help and rotate (switch). All players must maintain vision, ball-you-man, and be talking.

In diagram (i) & (ii), X3 is helping X2 on O2's dribble penetration. X1 must "help the helper" i.e. X1 will now defend O3.

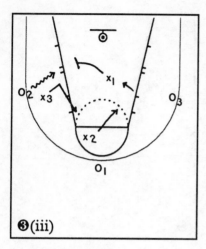

❸(iii)

3 on 3 Rotation (Contd.)

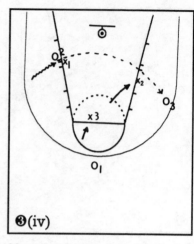

❸(iv)

O2 now makes skip pass to O3.
Defence must adjust.

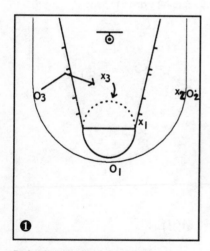

❶

❷

Defending the Flash Post/Cutter.

X3 must 'bump' the offensive man mid way across the lane. X3 will have his hand and foot nearest the ball, in the passing lane.
(In this example, left hand, left foot).
In the second diagram, X3 will either open to the ball or deny with right foot & right hand in passing lane.
('Snap' head).

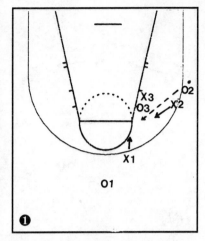 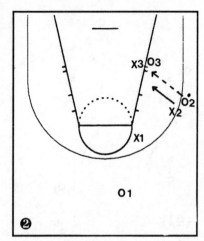

Defending the Entry Pass into Post.

X2 will make a half turn and slide down to try to slap ball away. (Especially if 03 puts ball on the floor).

(High post entry). X2 and X1 will 'harass' 03. ('Sink up on the post').

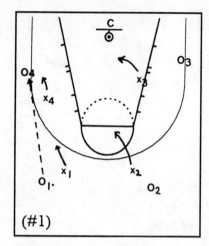

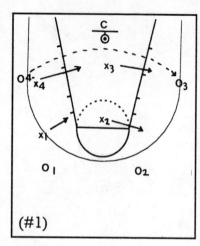

Shell Drill. (4 on 4).

Ball is passed only on Coach's command. Defence must adjust. They must talk, have hands up, react etc. all the time.

Progressions: #1. Offensive players pass ball wherever and whenever they like.
#2. Each offensive player must dribble in/dribble out left & right of his defender.
#3. The opposite forward to the ball cuts across the lane towards ball. (All offensive players now rotate).
#4. If pass is made guard to guard, passer screens down.

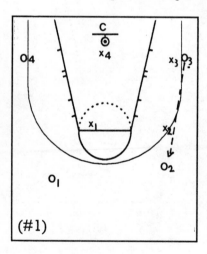

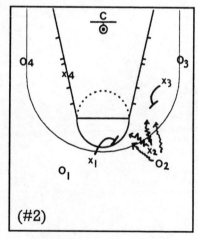

(Continued on next page)

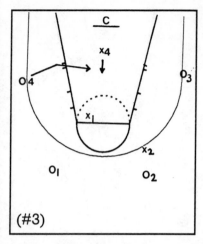

(#3)

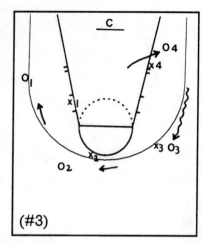

(#3)

#5. If pass is made guard to forward, passer screens away (lateral).
  6. Live four on four.

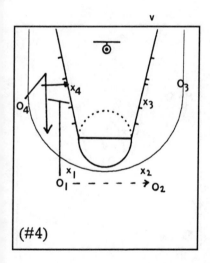

(#4)

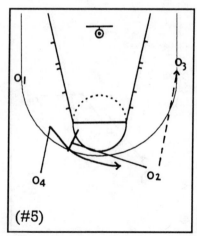

(#5)

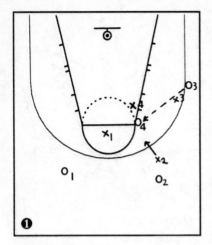

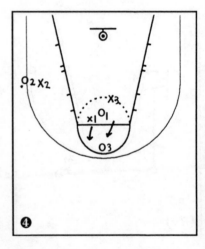

4 on 4 Post Defence.

High Post – X4 must be talking, X2 should sink up on the post.

Lost Post – X3 should be 'faking and bluffing' i.e. sliding in between O3 and O4.

Help Defence vs Screen Away.

X1 should "hedge" i.e. place a denying arm up in front of O3 as he comes off O1's screen, to discourage the pass. However, X3 should try to get over the pick so X1 can stay with O1 who can easily 'slip' the screen and cut to basket.

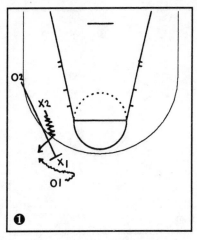

❶

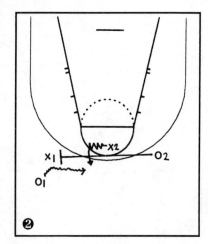

❷

Help defence vs On ball Screen.

X2 must move up (hedge) on the dribbler, giving vocal warnings.

X2 must be able to stop a drive by O1.

X2 must be able to close out on a shot by O1.

X2 must be able to front O2 to prevent a pass on O2's roll to basket.

X2 is trying to make the dribbler take a wider path (away from basket).

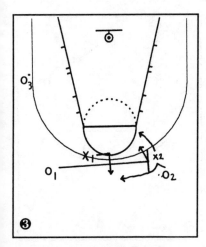

❸

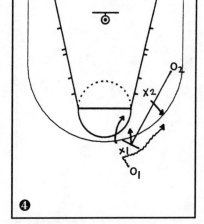

❹

Switching Drills. (Away from ball).

The screener's defender calls the switch. He must do it EARLY! Therefore in the diagram above. X1 will yell "Switch" and cover. O2 off the screen.

Switching Drills. (On the ball).

Here, X2 will yell "Switch" and cover O1.

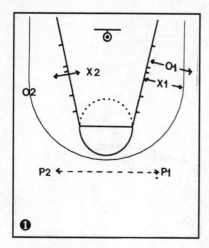

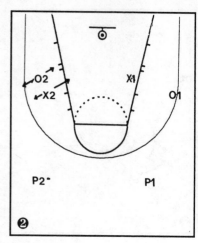

2 on 2 Helpside Drill.

P1 and P2 pass the ball between themselves 2 or 3 times. X1 and X2 are moving, sliding, talking according to position of ball.

P1/P2 then enter to wing, and O1/O2 go 2 on 2 vs X1/X2.

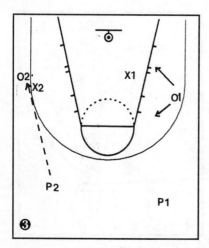

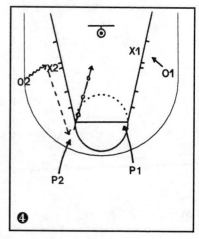

Progression: O1/O2 can kick it back out to P1/P2 for jump shot, then X1 and X2 must block out on O1 and O2.

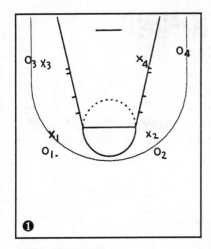 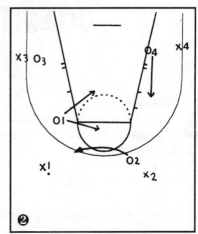

Indiana Knight Drill.

Play half court 4 on 4 or 5 on 5. When Coach blows whistle the Os put the ball on the floor. The Xs pick it up and attack the same basket. However O1 now cannot guard the ball, the defence must communicate and rotate to successfully defence the play.

CONDITIONING

1 SUICIDES
Sprint from baseline to free throw line and back, to 10 second line and back, to opposite free throw line and back, to opposite baseline and back.

All players aim for 30 seconds.

Pro's and National League 26–28 seconds.

2 WIND SPRINTS
Sprint baseline to baseline and back in 9 seconds.

3 3 MAN CONTINUOUS FAST BREAK
Everyone must make a lay up without the ball touching the floor and without a travelling violation. If you miss you keep going starting from zero.

4 4 MAN CONTINUOUS FAST BREAK
As #3.

5 4 MAN OR 5 MAN FAST BREAK
Make 10 lay ups going end to end in ONE minute. (Or 5/6 in 30 secs.)

6 1 ON 1 FULL COURT
Play full court one on one – winner is first to e.g. 3 baskets. Can have alternating possessions or make and take or "scrap" – i.e. whoever gets it out of net goes the other way on offence.

7 17 IN A MINUTE
Sprint sideline to sideline; all players must make 17 trips in less than one minute (from one side to the other sideline = 'one').

8 FULL COURT TIPPING
Two lines, one at each end, keep the two basketballs up on the backboards for e.g. 2, 2½, 3 minutes. If a ball touches the floor – clock starts again from zero. Players, after they jump up and tip ball, turn to their right and sprint to other end to join back of line.

9 FULL COURT TIPPING KILLER

As #8 except perform 2 push ups at mid court!

10 PASSING – DENIAL CONDITIONER

Use full court 5 on 5 or 6 on 6. No dribbling allowed except one dribble to improve passing angle. Blue team must try to make 15 consecutive passes. White team must try to deny all passes and get an interception or violation. (Also reward deflections). If blue team makes target, white team do push ups or sprint. You cannot pass back to the person who just passed to you.

11 DON'T MISS THE LAY UP

2 players pass the ball back and forth up the court. Each player must make 5 lay ups at full speed. If one is missed, start again from zero.

12 SLIDING/CONDITIONING KILLER

(i) Forward & backward sliding × 3.
(ii) Sideways sliding × 3.
(iii) Squat jumps or backboard/rim touches × 3.

Squad lines up on sideline. Blue team in one half, white team in the other. On the whistle blue team start sliding for 30 secs. (40 if desired). Coach keeps time, whistle blows, white team immediately begin, blue team rest and go back to starting spots. After 30 secs. whistle goes, blue begin, white rest etc.

13 JUMP AND BE QUICK DRILL

Player sprints from foul line to backboard, makes vertical jump to touch BOTH hands on rim (or backboard for shorter players), land, sprint back to foul line, touch line with foot, repeat. Drill last for 30 seconds. Go for a score of 9 trips.

14 BILLY THE KID DRILL

One player goes from end to end dribbling the basketball FULL SPEED. He must pull up outside the lane, and shoot the jumper. There is a rebounder under each basket who collects the ball and makes an outlet pass. The player MUST receive the pass within the 3 point line. He continues end to end until he has scored e.g. 10 baskets.

15 PHANTOM FUNDAMENTALS CONDITIONER

Players line up along baseline and begin V cutting from side to side up the floor and back. On the whistle (or Coach's command) perform the following. Each fundamental can be performed for 30 secs. or 1 minute then the Coach will explain the next one. Or you can have the players go up and back twice on each one.

After executing the required fundamental on the whistle the players continue to V cut till they hear the whistle again.

(i)   Jump stop reverse pivot left.
(ii)   Jump stop reverse pivot right.
(iii)   Jump stop front pivot left.
(iv)   Jump stop front pivot right.
(v)   Jump stop jab fake left.
(vi)   Jump stop jab fake right.
(vii)   Phantom rebound and outlet pass.
(viii) Phantom jump shot.
(ix)   Screen away and open to ball.
(x)   Backward sliding.
(xi)   Foot fire.
(xii)   Speed dribble left.
(xiii) Speed dribble right.
(xiv)   Dribble and cross over dribble.
(xv)   Sprint 5 yards.

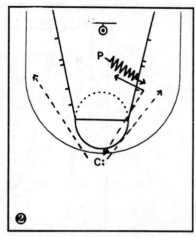

Pick Up Drill.

Coach rolls a ball away from player – player must move quickly to retrieve ball and return to Coach. Player goes back to starting point. Coach will roll a second ball out.
Start slow then get faster.

Pick Up Drill – Sliding!

Similar to previous drill, except Coach & player have changed positions and now player must defensive slide to retrieve ball.

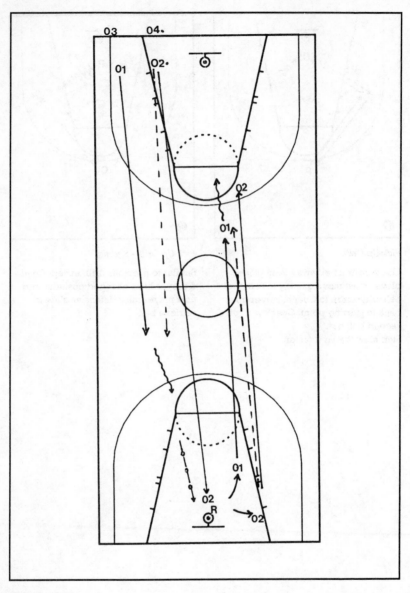

Blow Out Drill.

O2 throws a lob pass trying to make it land between the circles. O1 must catch it before it bounces twice and lay it up. O2 must get to other end to rebound ball before it bounces twice & repeat drill coming the other way.

4 successful trips then out.

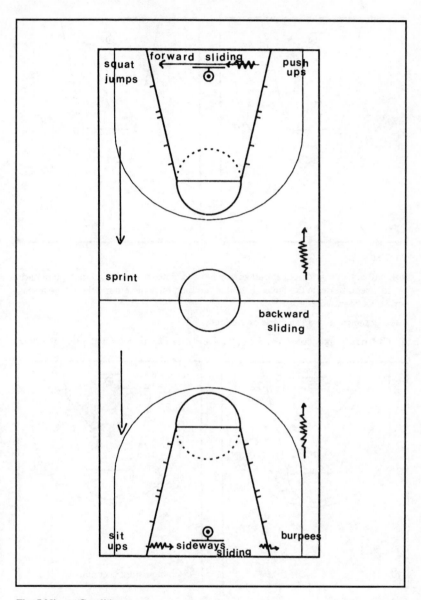

The 5 Minute Conditioner.

Players perform 10 reps of each exercise in each of the four corners whilst moving around the court using the methods shown on the diagram. Keep going for 5 mins.

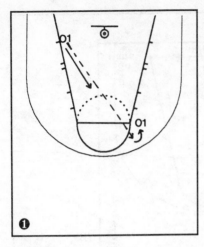

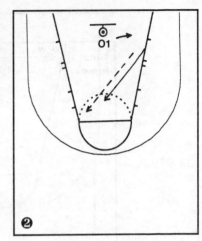

Box Drills.

Roll ball out with sufficient speed so you have to chase it, catch it, chin it, pivot and triple threat, perform the move, rebound the ball, hustle to other side of lane and repeat same move.

Keep going for e.g. 30 seconds or 1 minute.

(i) Jab & go. (ii) Jab, crossover & go. (iii) Fake drive & shoot. (iv) Fake shot & drive.

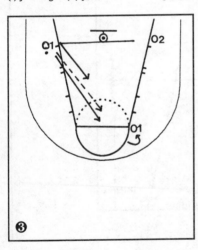

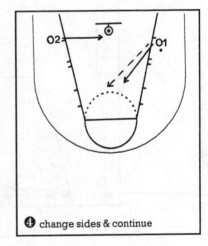

❹ change sides & continue

2 Man Box Drills.

As above except O2 does not have a ball. As soon as O1 starts to roll ball out, O2 goes across paint, touches lowest hash mark and gets ready to play defence on O1. Go 1 on 1, one shot, go to other side & repeat.

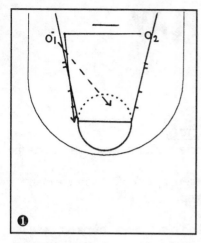

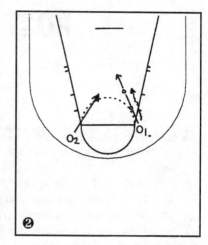

Box Drills (Contd.)

Block shot option: As before except now O2 must touch points as shown above, he then tries to block O1's lay up shot using the inside hand. i.e. left hand block shot for the right hand lay up on right side, and vice versa.

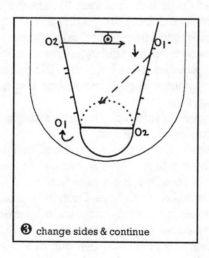

❸ change sides & continue

POST PLAY

Ten Back to the Basket Moves

1 Spin ball out for yourself each time. Perform hook shots inside the lane.

2 Challenging the defence: Drop step to 'lock off' defensive man.
Right hand shot = left leg drop step.
Left hand shot = right leg drop step.

3 From the side of the lane: Baseline pivot, shoot (or pass), read the defence (i) Outside (or inside) pivot, cross over (if defence plays tight), 'lock him off with cross over leg', 1 dribble across lane, hook shot.
(ii) Lane pivot (outside/inside turn), cross over towards hoop, 1 dribble, pump fake and power lay up.

4 From foul line: Outside pivot (left and right), shoot. Versus defence, read the defence first then, (i) Fake the jumper and drive (left and right), one dribble, step in direct line to hoop.
(ii) Cross over and drive. Pivot, fake jumper, cross over leg (swing ball away from the defence), drive to hoop.

5 Missed shot, rebound, pivot, hook shot. (No dribble).

6 From 'elbow' of lane: Vertical move; lane ball fake, drop step, 1 dribble, pump fake, shoot.

7 Horizontal move; outside ball fake, drop step (into lane), 1 dribble (between wide base), hook shot.

8 Vertical move – horizontal move: Lane ball fake, drop step, dribble down the lane, reverse dribble at lowest hash mark, (same hand), across lane, 2 steps, hook shot.

9 Horizontal move – vertical move: Outside lane ball fake drop step into lane, dribble (as though going across), reverse dribble (outside forearm parallel to floor), hook shot.

10 Loose ball reaction pivot: Roll ball out, pick it up, pivot, score. (Use cross over, power, hook, dunk – read the defence).

Perform all the above 1 on 0 first, then 1 on 1.

Inside Power Moves

"Malone"

(i) In the low post; player can either be there already, or he can flash/cut into the post from the opposite side. Coach is on the wing with ball ready to feed post.
Meet the ball, locate the defence, pass back. (Baseline foot must be positioned on block).

(ii) Meet the ball, drop lower foot towards the rim, pivot on heel of top foot towards the rim, pivot on heel of top foot, keep knees bent and head up. Keep your back facing the basket at the other end and your shoulders parallel to the baseline. Dunk shot or use glass.

(iii) Using power dribble: As you step in and toward the rim, make a two handed, one bounce power or 'crab' dribble in between the feet of your wide base. Don't straighten up until you are ready to shoot. Keep eyes fixed on the basket. Use your upper body to lift and protect ball as you power it up towards the goal.

"Wilkins"

(i) Meet the ball, pivot on lower foot, step, heel-toe towards the middle of the lane and as close as you can to the rim. Balance.

(ii) Take off foot should be parallel to the baseline and perpendicular to the sideline. 'Climb the ladder' with the other foot. Bring ball up from the thigh in one motion. Shoot the hook or baby hook.

(iii) Using power dribble: As for Malone only here be aware to protect the ball even more, as you are turning into the middle of the lane.

"Sikma"

(i) Meet the ball, pivot right and shoot the jumper.

(ii) Pivot left and shoot.

(iii) Pivot either way and shoot.
Stress: Stay at the same height when you turn as when you catch the ball.
Turn away from the pressure.
Use the bank shot as often as possible.

"McHale"

(i) Pivot to the baseline, pump fake, then crossing over, come 'up and under' towards the middle to shoot the jump hook, or baby hook.

(ii) Pivot to the inside, pump fake, then as (i).
Move in the direction opposite the pressure.

Seal or Pin

Utilize the 'arm bar' to keep defender out of the passing lane. Keep him 'on your back'.

Spin and seal according to ball movement.

Show target hand.

Maintain contact with the defender until the last possible moment before catching the ball.

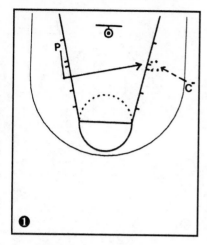

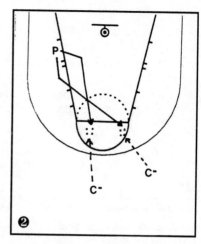

1 on 0 in the Post.

Post player must flash into the post (low and high), machine gun feet for 5 beats, post up strong, show target hand, receive pass and make the designated move.

Work both sides.

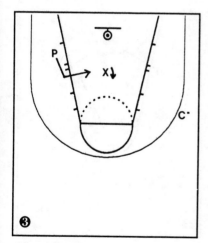

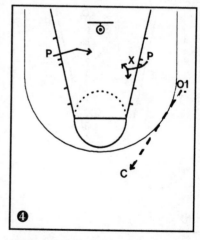

Add defence.

e.g. for spin and pin move, or seal the defensive player.

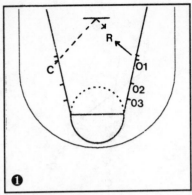

①

Post Offensive Rebound Drill.

Coach throws ball up off board,
1. O1 rips ball down and chins it, explodes back up for score.
2. O1 rips and chins, pump fake & power.
3. O1 rebounds, keep ball above head and go up quickly.
4. O1 rips & chins, power dribble from one side of rim to the other & go up strong.

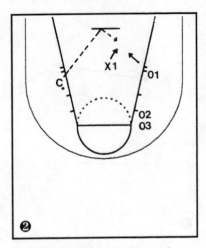

②

Post Offensive Rebound with muscle.

As before except introduce first one then two defensive players to "body" O1 as he tries to score.

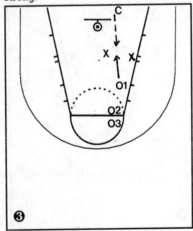

③

Be Aggressive Drill.

Coach is out of bounds, when he slaps the ball, O1 cuts in between the 2 defensive players. Coach rolls ball or bounce pass it or air pass. O1 must get ball and go up strong to basket without getting ball stripped.

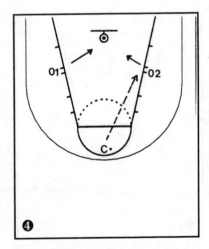

④

React & Be Quick Drill.

Coach can pass to either post player (both straddling the lane). The one who gets it attacks the basket quickly and aggressively. The other player becomes a defender and attempts to block the shot.

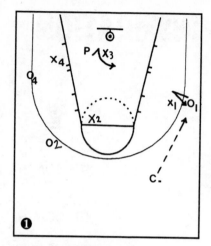

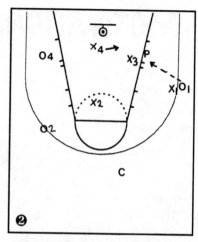

Inside-Out Post Man Drill.

Coach enters to wing. Ball must go inside to post man.
Coach will have huddled with defensive players to assign one X to double-down on the post. Post man must locate the open man, pass to him for a shot. Coach will designate a series of 'doublers'.

❶

❷

e.g. First 2 times, X4 will double, then X1, last 2 times it will be X2.

MOTIVATION/INSPIRATION

The Coach

Who loses the important game?	THE COACH.
Who has to shoulder all the blame?	THE COACH.
Who to teach the boys to play is hired	
And yet if one of them grows tired	
And fails to score is promptly fired?	THE COACH.
Who character is asked to build?	THE COACH.
With customers to keep the stadium filled?	THE COACH.
Who plans formations, old and new,	
And tells the youngsters what to do,	
But if they can't, is told: "You're through?"	THE COACH.
Who is by thousands second-guessed?	THE COACH.
Is jeered for plays he thought were best?	THE COACH.
Who has my deepest sympathy?	
Who is it I'd not care to be?	
Regardless of his salary?	
THE COACH.	

Attitude starts with an 'A'. It comes first.

Don't be discouraged by your size, champions come in all sizes.

Each player assumes that he has certain limits to his ability; usually this assumed limit is not sufficient to carry out his assignments.

Dedication and devotion are keys to success.

Valuable things in life don't come free, are you willing to pay the price?

You always become tired mentally before physically.

The guy who complains about the way the ball bounces usually dropped it.

The mark of a true champion is the one who can conquer the fear of making mistakes.

A rebound is your chance to score.

He who controlleth the backboard, controlleth the game.

When you're through improving, you're through.

No-one ever drowned in their own sweat.

If what you did yesterday still looks big today, then you haven't done much today.

By failing to prepare yourself, you are preparing to fail.

Winners are workers.

Good, better, best; never let it rest until your good is better and your better best.

Success is 99% perspiration and 1% inspiration.

A quitter never wins, a winner never quits.

Hustle; you can't survive without it.

Give me five men who hate to lose and I'll give you a winner.

It's not the size of the dog in the fight, but the size of the fight in the dog.

Lazy feet cause fouls.

Winning isn't everything, but losing is nothing.

Winning is the second step. Wanting to is the first step.

Hustle and desire make a winning team.

Aim for the stars and if you don't reach them you'll land pretty high anyway.

Teamwork plus desire = success.

There is no 'I' in team.

Teamwork means success – work together, win together.

Talent is God-given, conceit is self-given, be careful.

What good is skill without desire?

Ask not what your team can do for you, but what you can do for your team.

The difference between champ and chump is U.

Are you the answer to our problems, or are you a part of them?

Position for athlete and Christian: knees bent, head up.

It's best to remain silent and be thought a fool than to open one's mouth and remove all doubt.

Progress always involves risk.
You cannot steal second base and keep you foot on first.
It's a funny thing about life, if you refuse to accept anything but the best, you very often get it.

The winner and the loser: The winner says "It may be difficult but it is possible". The loser says "It may be possible but it is too difficult".

Every job is a self-portrait of the person who did it. Autograph your work with excellence.

The quality of a person's life is in direct proportion to their commitment to excellence, regardless of their chosen field of endeavour.

A wise leader is someone who picks smart people to work for him and then is smart enough to let them go out and do their job.

The will to win has always been overrated as a means of doing so. The will to prepare and the ability to execute are of far greater importance.

On having commitment not just involvement: "I had bacon and eggs this morning, now the chicken that provided the egg had involvement, but the pig that provided the bacon was COMMITTED".

THE PRICE OF SUCCESS
by Bob Holland

I often wonder what it is that brings one man success in life, and what it is that brings mediocrity or failure to his brother.

The difference can't be in mental capacity; there is not the difference in our mentalities indicated by the difference in performance. In short, I have reached the conclusion that some men succeed because they cheerfully pay the price of success, and others, though they may claim ambition and a desire to succeed, are unwilling to pay that price.

AND THE PRICE IS

To use all your courage to force yourself to concentrate on the problem in hand, to think of it deeply and constantly, to study it from all angles, and to plan.

To have a high and sustained determination to put over what you plan to accomplish, not if circumstances be favourable to its accomplishment, but in spite of all adverse circumstances which may arise – and nothing worth while has ever been accomplished without some obstacles having been overcome.

To refuse to believe that there are any circumstances sufficiently strong to defeat you in the accomplishment of your purpose.

Hard? I should say so. That's why so many men never attempt to acquire success, answer the siren call of the rut and remain on the beaten paths that are for beaten men. Nothing worth while has ever been achieved without constant endeavour, some pain and constant application of the lash of ambition.

That's the price of success as I see it. And I believe every man should ask himself: Am I willing to endure the pain of this strugle for the comforts and the rewards and the glory that go with achievement? Or shall I accept the uneasy and inadequate contentment that comes with mediocrity? Am I willing to pay the Price of Success?

AND THE TIME TO BEGIN TO PAY IS NOW.

MANAGEMENT PRINCIPLES

Applicable to Coaching

1 We don't discover our greatest potential. We DECIDE on it.
2 Catch people doing something right, or nearly right.
3 People who feel good about themselves produce good results.
4 Regard everyone as a potential winner.
5 Success by the inch is a cinch, by the yard is hard.
6 Success is often dependent, not on doing amazing brilliant things, but on doing the commonplace unusually well.
7 Recognize the attitude demotivators.
8 Seeing ourselves progressing motivates.
9 Challenge only motivates if we can win.
10 Group belonging motivates.
11 Show (players) how being goal orientated develops drive and will-power.
12 Explain positive thinking and its uses.
13 Make sure players realise that it is DESIRE NOT ABILITY that makes people succeed.

On Leadership

"I" Syndrome: The Coach who claims all the honour for the work of his team is sure to be met by resentment. The effective leader claims none of the honours but ensures, when there are any, that they go to his team.

A determination to fight for it: Nothing worth achieving is ever easy. The successful leader has a determination to achieve his goals no matter what obstacles come along. He believes in what he is doing and uses the maxim – unless we stand for something, we fall for anything.

The leader plans his work and works his plan.

The Coach who wavers in his decisions shows he is unsure of himself.

The successful leader understands every detail of HIS job.

Winning & Losing

A winner makes mistakes and says "I was wrong". A loser says "It wasn't my fault".

A winner credits his good luck for winning even though it wasn't luck. A loser credits his bad luck for losing, but it wasn't luck.

A winner goes through a problem and a loser goes around it.

A winner shows he's sorry by making up for it. A loser says he's sorry but he does the same thing next time.

A winner says "I'm good, but not as good as I ought to be". A loser says "Well, I'm not as bad as a lot of other people". A winner looks up to where he is going. A loser looks down at those who've not yet achieved the position he has.

A winner respects those who are superior to him and tries to learn from them. A loser resents those who are superior to him and tries to find fault.

Progressive Thinking

1   Do I appraise my work/private/social life, with "How can I do it better?"
2   Am I worth more as a person today than last week?
3   Am I following an organised personal development programme to increase my value to others?
4   Am I setting an excellent example for those I work with?

Final Thoughts ...

1   Set a high goal and go for it – this inspires everyone.
2   Expect to be judged by results.
3   Expect to be criticised – it's proof we're growing.
4   Do something different tomorrow.

BASKETBALL ALPHABET

A is for Anticipation, be ahead of the rest.
B is for the Ball, Boxing out and Being the Best.
C is for Charge when you get in that lane.
D is for Defence, 80% of the game.
E is for Effort, strive to be great.
F is for the Foul, when you get there too late.
G is for Guts when you dive for the ball.
H is for Hustle and Helpside which should be played by all.
I is for Intensity, be ready and set.
J is for the Jump shot, swish through the net.
K is for Keeping fit and staying in shape.
L is for Laziness, Last, Losing, everything I hate.
M is for Motivation, Mobility, Movement, you need them all.
N is for Nobody but me is gonna get that loose ball.
O is for Offence, play it tight and clean.
P is for Passing, play as a team.
Q is for Quickness, be alert and aware.
R is for Rebound, be strong in the air.
S is for Steal when you take the ball away.
T is for Turnover, don't make them when you play.
U is for Uniform, have pride in the way you appear.
V is for Victory that must be clear.
W is for Work and Win, they go hand in hand.
X marks the spot from where you shoot then land.
Y is for the Youth that's here today.
Z is for Zeal now go out and play.